W9-BYA-424

Willoughbyland

Also by Matthew Parker

The Battle of Britain
Monte Cassino
Panama Fever
The Sugar Barons
Goldeneye

Willoughbyland

England's Lost Colony

MATTHEW PARKER

Thomas Dunne Books
St. Martin's Press
New York

THOMAS DUNNE BOOKS.
An imprint of St. Martin's Press.

www.thomasdunnebooks.com
www.stmartins.com

Designed by Carrdesignstudio.com

Library of Congress Cataloging-in-Publication Data

Names: Parker, Matthew, author.
Title: Willoughbyland : England's lost colony / Matthew Parker.
Description: First U.S. edition. | New York : Thomas Dunne Books/St. Martin's Press, 2017. | "First published in Great Britain by Hutchinson, a Penguin Random House company"—Title page verso. | Includes bibliographical references and index.
Identifiers: LCCN 2016054215| ISBN 9781250112835 (hardcover) | ISBN 9781250112842 (e-book)
Subjects: LCSH: Suriname—History—To 1814. | Suriname—Colonization—History. | Willoughby of Parham, Francis Willoughby, Baron, 1613?–1666. | Great Britain—Colonies—America—History—17th century.
Classification: LCC F2423 .P37 2017 | DDC 988.3/01—dc23
LC record available at https://lccn.loc.gov/2016054215

Our books may be purchased in bulk for promotional, educational, or business use. Please contact your local bookseller or the Macmillan Corporate and Premium Sales Department at 1-800-221-7945, extension 5442, or by e-mail at MacmillanSpecialMarkets@macmillan.com.

First published in Great Britain by Hutchinson, a Penguin Random House company

First U.S. Edition: April 2017

10 9 8 7 6 5 4 3 2 1

In loving memory of David Parker
di tata di mi ta luku koni fu libi
di tata di mi ta hangi té

CONTENTS

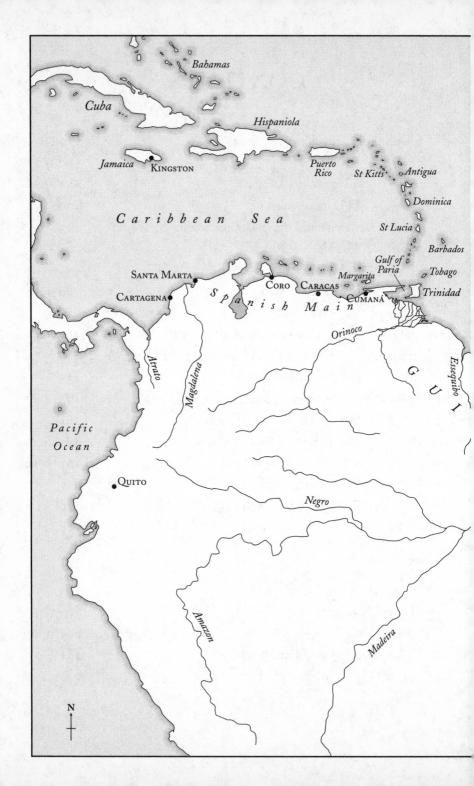

A t l a n t i c   O c e a n

Cayenne

Suriname

Wiapoco

A N A

Amazon

•BELÉM

Tocantins

B R A Z I L

NATAL•

RECIFE•

SURINAME RIVER, 2014

It is very hot and very strange. There's dense, relentless jungle on both sides of the broad mud-coloured river, massive trees festooned in thick vines. I'm looking for traces that might have been left behind by the English pioneers and refugees who, fleeing the turmoil of the English Civil War, built in Suriname what at one time looked to be the empire's most promising colony. I'm hoping that coming here will give me insight into what that adventure meant for those English men and women in the seventeenth century, and what it means to us now.

On my lap in the narrow canoe I have a map from 1667, showing plantations side by side all along the riverbanks. Most are named after their owners – Byam, Banister, Marten, Allin, Oxenbridge. But absolutely no traces remain; the jungle has reclaimed all their endeavours.

Suddenly, rounding a bend, we see some huts perched on an island midstream. It is a newly built lodge for visitors drawn by the beauties and wildlife of the unspoilt tropical jungle. There's even a small swimming pool for those unwilling to brave the caimans and piranhas of the river. But it is otherwise rudimentary: we are shown the viper's nest under the small dining area as a giant iguana slouches past; the electricity generator goes off at ten and I lie on my narrow bunk in the dark, sweating profusely, listening to the loud squeaking of bats in the beams above my head, while what sounds like a fight to the death between creatures unknown occurs on top of the roof. On the trunk of a tree just outside, a large tarantula sits unmovingly brooding, like a big, black disembodied hand.

The next day we set off again. Above us, massive vultures circle, as if expecting a disaster. Even early, it is ferociously hot. Then there is a sharp fall of rain, refreshing and cooling. When it stops, the river water begins to steam, till all around us is a thick mist. This place feels stranger and more unworldly than ever. We slow down, but then the steam clears and we press on once more upriver.

One

'EVERY MAN'S LONGING'

'There is a way found to answer
every man's longing'

SIR WALTER RALEGH ON GUIANA

At the beginning of the 1650s, England was in ruins – wrecked, impoverished, grief-stricken. Before the final victory of Parliament over the King in the Civil War some 80,000 soldiers had perished, out of a population that probably numbered fewer than 1.5 million males between the ages of sixteen and fifty. In all British history, only the First World War killed a larger proportion of the country's population. Another 100,000 men, women and children had perished from disease or hunger in besieged, often plague-ridden towns. Survivors had gone mad from shock and grief.

At the end of the war, crippled soldiers and beggars wandered everywhere, and many towns were shattered. A huge amount of the nation's wealth had already been expended – from Oxford college plate, to the shoes and bedding of the very poorest – but the end of fighting was followed by a period of serious slump, drastic price rises, heavy unemployment and deep hunger. At the same time taxes were almost seven times higher than they had been in the 1630s. To increase the misery still further, an intense period of cold set in after 1650, the deepest chill of the mini ice age.

But for the farmhand, slaving in the freezing rain of a Lincolnshire field, or the small-time tradesman, shivering in a garret room in a desolated town, there was an intoxicating fresh possibility. England had a new colony far away, in a place of 'Eternal Spring', as one report read, where the blissfully warm air was fragrant with the scents of oranges, lemons, figs, nutmeg and 'noble aromaticks'. The soil was 'luxuriant', producing trees of all types and in vivid colours, which 'appeared like nosegays adorn'd with flowers of different kinds'. This rich land teemed with 'strange rarities, both of beasts, fish, reptiles, insects, and vegetables, the which for shape and colour are wonderful.'

Living here – it was reported – were primitive peoples, happy to trade their plentiful gold, silver and pearls for trifles. For a good-quality knife, you could have ten times its value in tobacco or cotton, raw or woven into hammocks. Even better, they were extremely welcoming and friendly to the English, whose coming, they believed, was the fulfilment of a prophecy to rid them of Spanish oppression. Diseases? So rich and healthy was this region that locals lived up to one hundred and twenty years old. What's more, their women were the most beautiful in the world, as well as 'lascivious' and all 'nakedly expos'd to every wanton eye.'

This vision of paradise was called Willoughbyland, after its founder, and it was situated in Guiana in what is now Suriname, on the north-east coast of South America, about halfway between the great Amazon and Orinoco rivers.

Francis Willoughby, 5th Baron Willoughby of Parham, had fought for both sides in the Civil War, defecting to the Royalists in 1648. But most recently he had got himself appointed governor of the Caribbean islands and from his fastness in Barbados, the richest West Indian colony, had declared allegiance to the King just as the Royalist cause collapsed at home. He was soon thrown off the island by a victorious Parliamentary fleet, but not before he had prepared an exit strategy. At the surrender of the Royalist force at the Mermaid Tavern in Oistins, Barbados, in January 1652, it was agreed that Willoughby's fledgling settlement on the Suriname river, established on his orders and at his own (enormous) expense, 'shall be by him enjoyed and kept without any disturbance either of himself or those that shall accompany him thither.'

It was a settlement on the wildest, furthest frontier. While the mouths of the Orinoco and Amazon had been explored and settled by the Spanish and Portuguese respectively, the 900-mile space in between the two great rivers remained

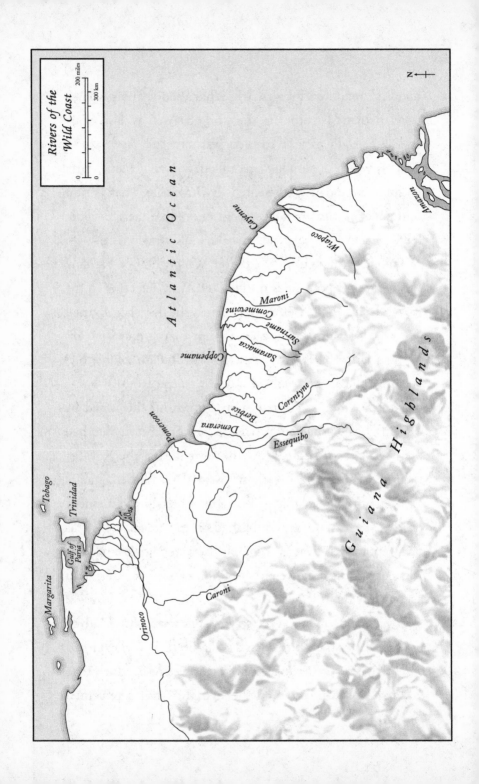

dark and unknown. Indigenous people called it Guiana, 'The Land of Many Rivers'. The Dutch referred to it as *de Wilde Kust*, 'The Wild Coast'. Early English explorers had labelled it 'Drownded Land', and almost lost count of the number of rivers reaching the sea along its coast. One reported fourteen, another forty. In fact, there are hundreds, carrying huge torrents of water out of the jungle, where up to three metres of rain falls each year. The largest are the Essequibo, Berbice, Suriname, Maroni and Wiapoco (also known as the Oyapoc). Although dwarfed by their giant neighbours, the Orinoco and Amazon, by European standards they are still vast; the mouth of the Essequibo river is almost as wide as the English Channel.

Behind the muddy, mangrove-choked shoreline lay deep swamps, and then thick forest of astounding vigour, size and strangeness. The French, when they came, called the Guiana interior *l'Enfer Vert*, 'Green Hell'. Far inland rise ancient flat-topped peaks. As the great rivers tumble off this high plateau they create massive, spectacular waterfalls.

In 1652, to the adventurous from the Caribbean islands or from home in England, the fledgling colony of Willoughbyland on the Suriname river offered freedom and independence – both religious and political – as well as exotic commercial and sensual possibilities. Willoughby himself gave further encouragement over the next three years, offering free land and cheap loans to new settlers and generous deals for indentured servants. Willoughbyland, declared its founder, was 'the sweetest place that was ever seen; delicate rivers, brave land, fine timber'. His advance party had stayed five months without anyone suffering so much as a headache, he wrote. Instead, they had enjoyed the pure air and water, and five meals a day from the plentiful 'fish and fowl, partridges and pheasants innumerable.'

Other parts of the West Indies offered enticing prospects to adventurers or exiles from England, particularly after sugar production had been established at the end of the 1640s. But Guiana had a special magic. Unlike the islands, it represented a huge expanse of land, most of it undeveloped, unexplored, unknown and mysterious (as, effectively, much of it remains today). One explorer described it as a virgin country, 'that hath yet her Maidenhead . . . never entered', a place untainted by the sins of the modern world. For Milton in *Paradise Lost*, it is an Edenic paradise, 'still unspoilt'. Indeed, Guiana had for some years been a byword for exotic eroticism, fertility and undiscovered riches. Shakespeare's Falstaff calls Mistress Page, a wealthy and sensual woman he intends to seduce, 'a region of Guiana, all gold and bounty'.

And it was gold or, more exactly, stories about it, that had first opened up the Wild Coast, and now offered the new settlers of Willoughbyland a tantalising prospect: that deep in the virgin jungle lay unimaginable riches in the form of a golden city, El Dorado.

Two

EL DORADO

'What do you not drive human hearts into,
cursed craving for gold!'

VIRGIL, *THE AENEID*

I T WAS Sir Walter Ralegh who had established a
fascination in England with Guiana. Fifty years before
the settlement of Willoughbyland, Ralegh had written *The
Discoverie of the Large, Rich and Bewtiful Empire of Guiana;
with a Relation of the great and golden city of Manoa, which the
Spanish call El Dorado.* The book was the result of a journey
made by the author to promote a new English imperial
adventure in South America, motivated by the quest for the
golden city of El Dorado. It was the publishing sensation of
its time, widely translated and frequently reprinted.

Ralegh writes of a fabulous city somewhere in the
hinterland of Guiana, called Manoa, standing on the shore
of a large lake, Parima. He even provided a map with lake
and city clearly delineated. The ruler was called El Dorado,
'the Gilded One', because of the ritual of covering him with

gold dust before he bathed in the lake, and this soon became the name of the imagined city. Ralegh located this site on a high plateau beyond the coastal jungles of Suriname, but never actually found it. He did, however, claim to discover mountains, 'thorough-shining, and marvellous rich'. Guiana, he announced, 'hath more abundance of gold than any part of Peru.'

El Dorado's origins go back to the very earliest European exploration of the Americas. On 31 July 1498, on his third voyage, Columbus, having been dangerously becalmed mid-Atlantic, landed on the southern coast of Trinidad to pick up much-needed water. He spent the next two weeks exploring the Gulf of Paria and the majestic delta of the Orinoco. Noticing that the river discharged fresh water far out into the ocean, he correctly surmised that he had found a great continent. He described the land as 'the loveliest in the world, and very populous'. Contacts with the indigenous people were friendly, and they 'came out in hordes to the ship, and many of them wore pieces of gold at their breasts . . . I spared no effort to find out where they obtained them.' He learnt, by means of signs and gestures, that the precious metal came from 'a high land, no great distance to the West', but across hard terrain made dangerous by cannibal tribes and venomous creatures.

The following year, under orders from the King of Spain, Alonso de Ojeda and Amerigo Vespucci sailed in search of this new continent, reaching the mainland somewhere on the Suriname coast. They were amazed by the size of the rivers and the huge clouds of silt that muddied the sea for leagues out from the shore. They did not see any inhabitants until they reached the Orinoco delta. Coming across indigenous dwellings on stilts over the mud flats of the river mouth, they called the area 'Little Venice' or Venezuela.

During this first rush of Spanish exploration, Vicente Yáñez Pinzón, who had sailed with Columbus, landed in what is now Brazil and then headed north, discovering the Amazon – which he thought might be the Ganges – before he too sailed along the Guiana coast. But low-lying mangrove swamps offered no obvious haven for further exploration of the interior. However, following a practice started by Columbus on his first voyage, local people were taken – willingly or not – back to Spain to learn Spanish so as to serve as interpreters on subsequent expeditions.

Everywhere in this region, the explorers came across rumours from locals of a golden city on high land deep in the interior of northern South America. A version of this story inspired the first inland exploration of South America by Europeans. In Darién, where Vasco Núñez de Balboa had established control and a small settlement, reports were heard of a place called Dabeiba, where there was believed to be a temple built entirely of gold. In 1512, Balboa led a search party up the Atrato river and then across land to within sight of the Andes. The following year he led a new expedition south-west which, though it produced no golden city, made him the first European to see the Pacific Ocean. Soon ships were launched and Spanish explorers and soldiers were pushing south along the coast towards Peru.

In 1520 Spanish conquistador Hernán Cortés marched into Tenochtitlan, the Aztec capital in Mexico. Confronted with the impressive buildings, great towers and fabulous treasures, 'Some of the soldiers,' one reported, 'asked whether the things we saw were not a dream.' So there was now a thrilling new inspiration for explorers: beyond even the most unpromising-looking coasts there might be mountains hiding kingdoms and advanced cities of unimagined and highly plunderable wealth.

During the following decade, Spanish settlements were established on the north coast of South America close to the Andes mountains. El Dorado, it was believed, was somewhere on a high plateau inland, directly to the south. This inspired, during the 1530s, a rapid process of discovery and conquest. The first expeditions were undertaken by German explorers: the Spanish King Charles V had granted Venezuela in virtual pawn to his German banker, the Welzer. On their orders, two separate expeditions set off south from Coro. Both were in the field for nearly three years, and lost three-quarters of their number to hostile indigenous people, disease or hunger.

But the golden city of El Dorado remained frustratingly out of reach. As the German explorers pressed forwards, the phantom goal seemed to retreat before them. According to local guides, relaying folk memory or myth, or just keen to have the Europeans off their patch, it was always round the next bend of river or just over the horizon.

In November 1533, Spanish conquistador Francisco Pizarro entered Cuzco, completing the military conquest of the Incan empire. Gold and silver started pouring out of Peru, stimulating rather than assuaging the appetite for further conquests.

And so, in April 1536, an expedition set off from Santa Marta on the Caribbean coast, hoping to find gold, of course, but also to investigate a route to Peru along the river Magdalena that would avoid the time-consuming crossing of the Panama isthmus. In command of 800 men was Gonzalo Jiménez de Quesada, a magistrate only recently arrived from Spain. A year later, he reached the foothills of the Andes with only 200 men surviving. There they came across sophisticated trade goods such as salt and textiles, alerting them that a superior civilisation might be close.

The stories told to the explorers often included details of how the inhabitants of El Dorado, like the Incas, were more 'civilised' than others – they wore clothes and lived in towns and cities. Most likely the rumours originated from the Musica people, a relatively sophisticated federation of clans on the high Colombian tableland around what is now the site of Bogotá. As per the El Dorado stories, their tribal chief did indeed have himself covered with gold dust, and, as an initiation rite, dive into a highland lake.

De Quesada fearlessly marched into the Musica realm and brought them to battle, entering their capital after defeating the army of the senior chief. Here they found much gold, including intricately worked pieces. But it was not El Dorado, the city of gold, and did not even have any rich mines, since the Musica obtained all their gold in trade. From prisoners they learnt that El Dorado did exist, but it was to the east.

Theodor de Bry's late sixteenth-century engraving of the ritual gilding of the fabled El Dorado.

The same story had been heard in Peru – that across the Andes was located a sophisticated civilisation in control of rich mines. The continuing search for this city, and consequently the exploration of the continent, thereafter moved from east to west.

New expeditions eastwards from the central Andes included that of Gonzalo Pizarro, the younger half-brother of Francisco. Francisco desired that Gonzalo should 'conquer such another land as [he] himself had found, and become governor of it'. On Christmas Day 1539, he led 340 Spaniards and some 4,000 press-ganged indigenous people east out of Quito. Second in command was his nephew Francisco de Orellana. But by the time they had left the mountains and entered the vast, soggy Amazon basin, 3,000 locals and 140 Spaniards had either died or deserted.

Pizarro now ordered the construction of a small brigantine, which Orellana was to take with fifty men on a river heading east; his instructions were to explore and then return with news. But when the river joined another flowing quickly east, a combination of the difficulty of returning against the current and the mutinous nature of the men persuaded Orellana to continue. Hostile tribes were fought off as the river received more and more tributaries and grew to a majestic size. Eventually, in August 1542, they reached the Atlantic: Orellana had completed the first known navigation of the entire Amazon river. Meanwhile Pizarro had staggered back to Quito, with only eighty men making it alive.

More northern expeditions chasing the El Dorado 'will-o'-the-wisp' eastwards suffered similar attrition, though without the compensation of Orellana's spectacular exploratory achievement. One, led by another German, Philipp von Hutten, set off from Coro in 1541 and soon found itself in 'a very sterile and pestilential land, with very few natives'. Starvation drove the men to eat ants, which caused them to suffer a strange ailment that turned them a sickly orange. 'Those afflicted grew desperate for salt and would seize any old piece of sweat-soaked clothing to eat it . . . Their hair fell out, and in its place emerged a pestilential scabies from which they died.'

Still, several Spanish would-be conquistadors were given royal patents to conquer El Dorado, and boldly set off from the Venezuelan coast. Hunger, disease, desertion and attacks by indigenous people brought all their efforts to their knees. On one expedition on the upper Amazon in the 1560s only twenty-five survived out of 2,000, its leader declaring, 'The reports are false. There is nothing on the river but despair.' All the time, however, the focus for the search moved eastwards. In 1576, an expedition led by Don Pedro Malaver de Silva landed on the Wild Coast between the Essequibo and Wiapoco rivers. Its complement included 160 men and its leader's two daughters. Nothing would be heard of their fate for a decade.

Those who did return sometimes brought back gold trinkets, or fresh details of the fabulous city picked up from local rumours. Almost all explained their failure not by doubting El Dorado's existence but by presuming it must be elsewhere. So the fabled location kept moving to the least explored part of the continent, settling at last in the mysterious tableland of Guiana, behind the Wild Coast.

While in the 1520s Spanish settlements were being established on the coast of what is now Venezuela and Colombia, and from the 1530s the Portuguese were colonising Brazil, the coast in between the Orinoco and Amazon rivers remained relatively free of European encroachment. There may have been a Spanish settlement at the mouth of the Essequibo in around 1530, but if so, it was certainly short-lived. In 1549, the governor of Hispaniola commissioned a Spanish nobleman to explore and colonise the region between the Orinoco and Amazon. But he failed to take advantage of the concession. As well as its muddy coasts and difficult currents, the area was inhabited in many places by warlike and aggressive people who would become known as Caribs or Cariba or Caniba, hence 'cannibal'. They were reportedly able to 'loose ten or a dozen arrows in the time it takes to load a gun', and the Spanish policy of slaughter and terror, effective elsewhere in cowering the indigenous peoples into submission, only prompted them to martial fury.

In 1568, a total of 126 families arrived at the mouth of the Cayenne river direct from Spain, but support from the Spanish towns established on the Main was extremely difficult because of the winds and currents, isolating the Cayenne settlement. Within five years they had gone, leaving no trace, presumably wiped out by hostile indigenous people or demoralised by disease and desertion.

The earliest English contact with the region was by privateers who appeared off the west coast of Trinidad and in the Orinoco delta at the close of the 1560s. But first to exploit the power vacuum of the Wild Coast were the Dutch. By 1580, they were established on the Pomeroon river, trading with the local people and doing a much better job of supplying the Spanish settlements than their own ships were able.

The previous year had seen the death of Jiménez de Quesada, the conqueror of the Musica. This feat had given him huge estates in New Granada from which flowed a great income in tribute gold, cotton and salt. All this he now bequeathed to his niece's husband Antonio de Berrío.

The family, including six young daughters and two infant sons, immediately set sail from Spain. Berrío was sixty, and a veteran soldier of battles in Italy, Germany and the Netherlands. Three of his brothers had died fighting for Spain on land or sea. When they arrived, Berrío discovered that his benefactor had inserted a clause in his will stipulating that he must devote his life and new fortune to continuing the quest for El Dorado. Berrío took on the task with relish, writing to the Spanish King in September 1583: 'May it please God to let this concealed province be discovered, and a great infinity of peoples be converted to the Catholic faith, and the royal patrimony be greatly increased, by the love of God!'

He immediately put his new riches to use, spending 30,000 ducats in raising and equipping a force of 200 men with a great quantity of horses, cattle, ammunition and stores. In 1584 he set out from his domain in the Andes, following rivers that eventually reached the Orinoco as it flowed past the edge of the Guiana Highlands. Seventeen months later he was back in New Granada having lost half his men and found nothing but trinkets and more rumours.

Undeterred, he returned to the Orinoco the following year with another large expedition. This would last nearly two and a half years as the east bank of the Orinoco was searched for the elusive pass through the mountains that guarded the city of El Dorado. For Berrío, who called himself the Gobernador de la Provincia del Dorado, the quest had become an obsession, and the Marquisate of El Dorado, the third after Mexico and Peru, now seemed to him within reach. His surviving men were less convinced. Plagued with 'river blindness', caused by a parasite that lives in the Orinoco, and suffering strange hallucinations, most deserted, bringing yet another expedition to an end.

Back in Bogotá, Berrío heard a story that reinvigorated his hope once more. Earlier in 1586, a Spaniard, Juan Martínez de Albujar, stumbled out of the jungle around the Orinoco river with an extraordinary story to tell. Having been abandoned by de Silva's El Dorado expedition of 1576, (of which he turned out to be sole survivor) de Albujar had been rescued by indigenous people and then led, blindfold for fourteen days, to El Dorado, on Lake Parima. The city was so vast it took a day to walk across; it had long straight streets and its temples were full of golden idols. When he chose to leave, he was presented with as many gold pieces as he could carry. Unfortunately all but a few gold beads were stolen from him on his journey to the coast.

An entirely different version of the story was that he had simply lived among the primitive tribes of the Orinoco, learnt their language, fought for them in wars, and taken several wives. El Dorado, he told the authorities when he eventually reached Margarita, 'does not and never did have foundations'. Berrío had no hesitation about which version of this tale he wanted to believe, and as quickly as possible put together a third expedition to the Orinoco, this time with 220 horses, large amounts of supplies, rafts, canoes, porters and 100 Spaniards, including his son, Fernando, now aged twelve.

For a year they searched the upper reaches of the Orinoco before a disease 'like the plague' killed most of the porters and some thirty Spaniards. Then thirty-four absconded, taking most of the horses with them. To prevent further desertions, Berrío ordered the rest of the horses to be killed. The remaining men then completed the dangerous voyage down the Orinoco to the coast. At last Berrío arrived at Trinidad, with twenty survivors, all sick. Berrío too was feverish, and his sanity was beginning to unravel. He made his way to Margarita, where he learnt that his wife had died at home in New Granada.

But his epic journeys, and his heroic action of killing the horses in the middle of the unknown, had attracted the admiration of Domingo de Vera, a rich Spaniard living in Caracas. He met Berrío, and agreed to help. The first step was to establish a new settlement in Trinidad to act as a base from which to continue the quest. Vera duly achieved this in early 1593 and then, leaving Berrío in Trinidad, set off himself with thirty-five men up the Orinoco.

He travelled inland for a fortnight. Here he met a chief 'who calls himself Carapano', who told him that about 250 miles further inland was a high plateau with 'great towns and a vast population with gold and precious stones'. There was also a large salt lake where, twenty years before, a huge host of clothed people, who were great traders, had arrived and conquered the tribes on the southern side. Away to the west, the Spaniards were told, was a race of men 'whose shoulders were so high that they were almost on a level with the head'.

The origin of the story of 'Lake Parima' has now been identified as seasonal inland flooding, and there is evidence of the invasion or migration of a semi-civilised people, the Arkunas, traders who would have collected a quantity of gold. It is possible that their relative prowess and wealth was exaggerated by overawed surrounding tribes. Needless to say, however, this story was seen by Europeans through the prism of the El Dorado legends.

Two weeks later Vera was back in Trinidad, with the latest news of the location of Lake Parima, and bearing seventeen golden eagles and jackals, finely worked, that had supposedly originated in El Dorado itself. Berrío was delighted, declaring the gold of such workmanship that 'I know not whether the silver-smiths of Spain could fashion conceits so life-like and of such perfection.' The city on the lake was the centre of a new empire of Incas, Vera had decided, put together by those who had escaped from the ravages of Pizarro sixty years earlier. At least 1,000 men were needed to conquer it, he said. Vera returned to Spain to raise troops. But then disaster struck for Berrío: Sir Walter Ralegh arrived at Trinidad.

Three

RALEGH AND THE 'BEAUTIFUL EMPIRE OF GUIANA'

'To seek new worlds, for gold,
for praise, for glory'
SIR WALTER RALEGH, 'THE OCEAN TO CYNTHIA', C. 1592

Courtier, statesman, soldier, sailor, scientist and man of letters, Walter Ralegh was described by French historian Abbé Raynal as 'one of the most extraordinary men that ever appeared in a country abounding in singular characters . . . He was passionately fond of everything that was magnificent . . . [he] had a kind of romantic leaning in his sentiments and behaviour.' In fact, he was a brilliant man of ideas but a frequent failure in the sphere of action.

Walter Ralegh was born in around 1552 to a propertied and strongly Protestant Devon family, the youngest of five sons. After Oxford and the Inns of Court, he fought in France for the Huguenots. He made his name in Ireland during the suppression of a Catholic revolt from 1579 to 1583, where he missed no chance for self-promotion.

He returned to England to find himself in the perilous position of being Queen Elizabeth I's chief favourite. He was knighted and rewarded with lucrative state monopolies and estates in Devonshire. Fond of ostentatious displays of his new wealth, he soon garnered a reputation for greed and sharp financial practice.

Handsome, charismatic and tall – literally head and shoulders above most other men – Ralegh was also a tangled mixture of ambition and insecurity. He was outspoken, abrasive and deceitful, and made little effort to endear himself to the court. Soon he was widely loathed and distrusted. A contemporary described him as a man 'who had offended many and was maligned of most.' His following, however, was not at court, but among seafarers, map-makers and mathematicians.

After the death at sea in 1583 of his half-brother Sir Humphrey Gilbert, with whom he had sailed on at least one abortive mission to the Americas, Ralegh obtained a charter to 'discover, settle and govern any lands not already in the possession of a Christian Prince.' This effectively covered the American Atlantic coast to the north of the Gulf of Florida – the limit of Spanish expansion. Although the resulting efforts in Virginia – largely funded out of his own pocket – were unsuccessful, Ralegh can still be seen as the father of English colonisation of the Americas. Unlike Drake and Hawkins, he was a settler, with a vision of possession and empire rather than plunder. For him, America was not just a stopping-off point on the way to the riches of the East, but worth settling in its own right, to absorb surplus population, stimulate trade, and reduce unemployment. This comparatively benign imperial vision, so different from what was to come later, would survive beyond the founding of Willoughbyland, but not beyond its fall.

By 1592 Ralegh's position as Queen's favourite had been lost to Robert Devereux, 2nd Earl of Essex, and he was briefly imprisoned in the Tower when his secret marriage to Elizabeth Throckmorton, one of the Queen's ladies of the bedchamber, was discovered. Exiled from court, nearly bankrupt, and desperate to regain the favour of the Queen, Ralegh turned his attention to South America, and in particular the no man's land of Guiana.

For Ralegh, the Wild Coast offered the chance to attack Spain at the source of its wealth: did not the Orinoco river provide the means to conquer Peru from the east, and thus cut off Spain's supply of silver and gold, 'that endangereth and disturbeth all the nations of Europe'?

Guiana also offered something more immediately eye-catching for investors. Ralegh had heard about El Dorado and its wonders 'many years since', he later claimed. He might have been told about it by Pedro Sarmiento de Gamboa, a

Spanish explorer and naval commander captured at sea by one of Ralegh's captains in 1584. Then, in mid- or late 1593, there came into his hands letters captured from Spanish vessels by English sea captains. These included Berrío and Vera's most recent detailed reports on the supposed location of Manoa or El Dorado. For Ralegh, it seemed his moment had come to seize the rich prize for England, and thus regain the favour of his Queen.

His first move was to send Jacob Whiddon, 'a man most honest and valiant', who had sailed with him on privateering tours, to the Orinoco delta to 'get knowledge of the passages'. Whiddon had a major setback at Trinidad, where eight of his men were killed by Berrío's soldiers having been promised safe conduct on shore to collect water, but otherwise he returned in late 1594 with favourable reports. He also brought back four men, two from Trinidad and two from the mainland, to be trained as interpreters. This was usual practice and Ralegh's first reconnaissance of Virginia had done the same thing. These interpreters, who might have travelled back to England for a reward, out of curiosity or out of a wish to recruit the English against their Spanish oppressors, would be essential for Ralegh's quest.

On 6 February 1595, with five ships and just over a hundred men, Ralegh, aged in his early forties, set sail to gain a new empire for his country. The bulk of his remaining fortune was sunk in the venture. In late March he arrived off Trinidad, and managed, without anyone raising the alarm, to sail around the island, noting fresh-water sources and Spanish defences. He also landed two of the indigenous people from Whiddon's voyage, presumably those from Trinidad rather than the mainland. They made contact with local chiefs hostile to the Spanish usurpation of their island.

On 4 April, Ralegh sailed into what is now Port of Spain harbour and dropped anchor. He then sent Berrío a letter requesting a meeting, promising 'on a gentleman's honour that it will be in all security', with a ring and effigies of the Virgin and St Francis to assure the Spaniard of Ralegh's Catholic sympathies. Berrío, taken by surprise and with only about fifty men under his command, sent his nephew and eight soldiers, bearing fruit, chicken and venison, to try to discover the Englishman's intentions.

Ralegh's flagship raised a white pennant and the nephew and four of the men went aboard. Here they were plied with drink, as were the remaining four waiting on shore. When they were sufficiently intoxicated, all the Spaniards on board ship and on the beach were bound and then stabbed to death.

When Berrío, waiting in the new town of St Joseph five or so miles inland, had heard nothing for some hours he tried to rally his remaining men. But when four days later Ralegh's troops, together with indigenous allies, attacked the town, there was little resistance. Twenty Spaniards were killed and eleven captured. These were promptly executed and only Berrío and one other man were spared and taken as captives to Ralegh's ship. The fledgling town was burnt to the ground.

Now Ralegh demanded to be told the way to El Dorado. Berrío began by stressing the appalling difficulties of the jungle of the mainland, hoping to discourage Ralegh. When this failed to have the desired effect, he became vague and pretended ignorance. At one point, Ralegh took him ashore and threatened instant death if his memory did not immediately recover.

When Berrío saw that Ralegh was not to be placated he 'was stricken into a great melancholy and sadness'. For Berrío, a prize that had taken thirteen years of struggle, of risking death in the jungles from the Andes to the Atlantic, was being snatched away from him just as it looked within reach at last.

Leaving behind a small garrison and the larger ships, Ralegh took about a hundred soldiers and seamen in three shallow-bottomed boats, together with indigenous guides and translators from Trinidad, and following the route suggested by Berrío and Vera's captured reports, headed for the Orinoco delta on the mainland opposite Trinidad.

Even with the guides, it was a tricky journey through the 'broken lands and drowned lands' of the delta, where there were hidden shoals and strong currents. The boats were mainly rowed, though occasionally a sail was hoisted if the wind was favourable. And all the time the men were 'driven to lie in the rain and weather in the open air, in the burning sun, and upon the hard boards'. High trees on the banks kept the breeze from refreshing them. Soon they were 'wearied and scorched'.

But after about a week, the 'woods, prickles, bushes and thorns' on the riverbanks gave way to more open ground: 'plains of twenty miles in length, the grass short and green, and in divers parts groves of trees by themselves, as if they had been by all the art and labour in the world so made.' Deer came down to feed by the water's side, and brightly coloured water fowl were everywhere. It was, Ralegh later wrote, 'the most beautiful country that ever mine eyes beheld.'

At every stage of the journey, Ralegh noted details of the different tribes living on the riverbanks, and made every effort to meet their chiefs, particularly those who had had dealings with Vera. He was warmly received, partly on account of the 'notorious cruelties, spoils and slaughters' of the Spanish, but also because of the sharply contrasting behaviour of his men. They were forbidden to take so much as a pineapple without payment, and most important of all, the indigenous women were off limits. He later affirmed that none of his men 'by violence or otherwise, ever knew any of their women, and yet we saw many hundreds, and had many in our power, and those very young, and excellently favoured, which came among us without deceit, starke naked. Nothing got us more love among them than this usage.'

Ralegh also announced that he came from a great Queen, who was 'an enemy to the Spanish in respect of their tyranny and oppression, and that she delivered all such nations that were about her, as were by them oppressed.' Having freed the coast of the northern world from servitude to Spain, he said, she 'had sent me to free them also, and withal to defend the country of Guiana from their invasion and conquest.'

Such was the success of this approach that Ralegh was confident enough to declare that almost all of the tribal chiefs on the borders of El Dorado 'are already become her Majesty's vassals, and seem to desire nothing more than her Majesty's protection and the return of the English nation.'

Of the chiefs he describes, Ralegh was most impressed with Topiawari, who controlled the land around the junction of the Orinoco and Caroni rivers. On one of the Caroni's banks, Berrío had told Ralegh, was a 'great silver mine'. The river looped back to the east, so also offered a route to the Guiana highlands. Topiawari, Ralegh reported, was over a hundred years old, but was incredibly fit as well as full of information about the area and local tribes. 'I marvelled to find a man of that gravity and judgement, and of so good discourse,' Ralegh later wrote, 'that had no help of learning nor breed.' Topiawari repeated the story that El Dorado was peopled with Incas who had escaped Pizarro, and told

Ralegh with Topiawari, who arrived 'with many women and children, that came to wonder at our nation and to bring us down victual.'

Ralegh that the outskirts of this empire were only four days' march away, situated upriver on the Caroni.

The next day Ralegh reached the mouth of the Caroni, but now the rains had begun, swelling the waters. Once on the river, he found it impossible to make headway against the current. So he and his men made camp on the riverbank and began to look for silver- or gold-bearing rocks. Near a waterfall, they found some promising-looking specimens. Now, fearful that the rising waters of the Orinoco would be getting too dangerous to sail on, Ralegh headed back downriver. On the way he was told of a 'mountain of crystal' some fifteen miles away. He managed to see it, but because of the 'evil season of the year' could not reach it to investigate. Then, after further difficulties in the now torrent-like river, he eventually reached Trinidad.

Ralegh brought from the mainland 'two royal sons', one of whom was Cayowaroco, son of Topiawari. (Cayowaroco seems to have returned home two years later after the death of his father. Nothing is known of his time in England, but it is possible that he performed as an 'Indian Prince' in a 'devise' staged for Queen Elizabeth by the Earl of Essex.) In the place of the 'royal sons', Ralegh left with Topiawari two men, twenty-five-year-old Francis Sparrey 'who was desirous to tarry, and could describe a country with his pen', and sixteen-year-old Hugh Goodwin 'to learn the language'. It appears that Ralegh also took three more local men home, at least one of whom was coerced. Sparrey was later captured and taken to Spain where he endured a long imprisonment. Goodwin was hidden by the Indians who told the Spanish soldiers looking for him that he had been devoured by a jaguar. He would be found by Ralegh more than twenty years later, having almost forgotten how to speak English.

Disappointed with the meagre returns from his mainland expedition, Ralegh now decided to plunder towns on the Spanish Main, in order to gain at least some tangible profit for those who had helped finance the expedition. But he was turned away at Margarita and then suffered a severe defeat at Cumaná, losing as many as fifty men, including his cousin Grenville and Captain Calfield, one of his most senior officers. Efforts to ransom Berrío ended in failure also, and he was eventually exchanged for an English prisoner.

So the mission ended in disappointment and ignominy. Little had been achieved at great cost. Ralegh claimed that he had performed a great act of exploration. He did get 180 miles up the Orinoco, but it was familiar land to the Spanish who had been in Trinidad; hardly uncharted territory. Where Berrío's expeditions had taken years, Ralegh's took weeks. Virtually all his talk of El Dorado came not from his own exploration, but from captured Spanish sources of which he was far too trusting, just as later Englishmen would be too trusting of him.

Ralegh declared that Guiana 'hath more quantity of gold, by manifold, than the best parts of the Indies, or Peru.' But when tested in London, his samples of 'gold-carrying rock', gathered from Trinidad and the Orinoco, were dismissed as worthless. So support for his dreamt-of English colony in Guiana was not forthcoming from court. Some of his enemies even suggested that he had made the entire voyage up, while skulking in Cornwall, and that he was too 'easeful and sensual' to undertake such an adventure. Outraged by this suggestion, Ralegh sat down to write a book about his exploration.

Meanwhile, he organised a follow-up expedition, commissioning Captain Lawrence Keymis, an Oxford mathematician who had been on the first voyage, to continue the search and to maintain friendly relations with the indigenous people. Following the death of Jacob Whiddon on Ralegh's expedition, Keymis was now his most senior lieutenant. Keymis took with him 'John Provost, my Indian interpreter', who had been trained in Ralegh's household and might well have served as Ralegh's chief interpreter the year before having been originally picked up by Whiddon. Keymis was charged by Ralegh with finding a better route to the 'inland lake' and also instructed to collect more samples from the waterfall on the Caroni river. But Ralegh's incursion up the Orinoco had alarmed the Spanish, and soon after his departure Vera had brought 1,000 soldiers from Spain to re-garrison Trinidad and a new fortified settlement, San Thomé, very close to the junction of the Caroni and Orinoco rivers. Thus Keymis found his route to the waterfall blocked.

On the other part of his mission Keymis was more successful, sending a pinnace up the Essequibo river, collecting information from people there of a vast lake only a day's march from its headwaters. He also explored the Wiapoco and Maroni rivers, and venturing inland, he reported, he found a rich mine. On his return to England he told Ralegh that he would stake his life on being able to find it again. 'My self, and the remaining of my few years, I have bequeathed wholly to Raleana, and all my thoughts live only in that action,' he wrote at the end of his report on his voyage. 'I can discern no sufficient impediment to the contrary, but that, with a competent number of men, her Majesty may, to her and her successors, enjoy this rich and great empire.' Everywhere he had gone, Ralegh's name brought friendship from the local inhabitants who were impatient for him to return to help them against their mutual enemy, the Spanish. They would have many years to wait.

Ralegh's account of his expedition, published in 1596, is engaging, gripping, and extraordinary. At times, it reads a little rushed in the writing, but it is full of passion and arresting detail, whether it's his declaration at the beginning that 'in the winter of my life, [I] undertake these travails fitter for bodies less blasted with misfortune' or his description of the 'labyrinth of rivers' of the spectacular Orinoco delta or the heavy smoking of its inhabitants 'in the excessive taking thereof they exceed all nations'. At least four editions of his book appeared in England in the year of publication, and it was quickly translated into Latin, German, Dutch and French.

Above all, it is fascinatingly full of contradictions, an intriguing combination of rhetoric and record, the mundane and the fantastical, the pragmatic and the heroic.

Ralegh provides information of the make-up of local tribes – customs, trade patterns, even gender relations – still considered today as priceless anthropological evidence. But alongside this well-observed and credible detail there is patent hearsay, including a description of a tribe of people without heads, who had 'their eyes in their shoulders, and their mouths in the middle of their breasts'. Ralegh also can't resist writing of a tribe of Amazons, rich in gold but 'cruel and bloodthirsty', who defeated all male invaders, but once a year allowed men from nearby tribes to join them to 'feast, dance, and drink of their wines in abundance', then 'accompany them'.

Similarly, there is useful and practical information for potential settlers, on such things as rivers, food, climate and potential export crops. He notes rare woods and dyestuffs, and that 'all places yield an abundance of cotton, of silk, of balsamum . . . of all sorts of gums, of Indian pepper.' The soil is 'so excellent, as it will carry sugar, ginger, and all those other commodities which the West Indies have.' But alongside this, we have reports on the situation and history of the imagined empire of El Dorado, down to the smallest details. He writes that the Incas came from the west, wearing 'large coats and hats of crimson colour'. Their houses have 'great rooms, one over the other'. An earlier English visitor to Guiana had noticed 'a manifest desire to invest in all that related to the new continent the air of marvel.' In his book,

Ralegh speculates, without of course any evidence at all, that it 'be very likely that the emperor [of El Dorado] hath built and erected as magnificent palaces in Guiana as his ancestors did in Peru.' So, with little more than rumour and imagination, El Dorado takes shape on the page.

Like other writers on America, Ralegh sees and depicts Guiana as feminine and virginal. Charles V of Spain, he writes, 'had the maidenhead of Peru', but Guiana 'hath yet her Maidenhead . . . never sacked, turned, nor wrought; the face of the earth hath not been torn, nor the virtue and salt of the soil spent . . . It hath never been entered by any army of strength, and never conquered or possessed by any Christian prince.'

When Lawrence Keymis published his account of his follow-up voyage, there appeared in the preface a poem by George Chapman, which was probably commissioned by Ralegh as part of the pro-Guiana propaganda campaign. In Chapman's poem, Guiana is not only female, but subservient and willing:

> Guiana, whose riche feete are mines of golde,
> Whose forehead knockes against the roofe of Starres,
> Stand on her tip-toes at faire England looking,
> Kissing her hand, bowing her mightie breast,
> And every signe of all submission making

In the poem, England and her 'maide' are also feminine, but the 'soule of this exploit' is Ralegh with his 'Eliza-consecrated sworde'.

The poem, with its Latin title – 'De Guiana, Carmen Epicum' – and use of the epic form, aims to do for English colonialism in the Americas what Virgil did for Aeneas's adventures into Africa and Italy, colouring his exploits with a nationalistic, heroic hue. Chapman implores the Queen to back Ralegh and thereby 'create/A golden worlde in this our yron age'. This is both material – underwritten by real gold – and poetic. In the innocent nature of Guiana is to be found a pastoral prelapsarian idyll, unspoilt by the modern world. As in Elizabethan poetry, this is coloured by classical allusions. Ralegh is said to lead an 'Argolian Fleet', his quest for the gold of El Dorado likened to Jason searching for the Golden Fleece. In the same way, Ralegh's inclusion in his book of the stories of the headless men (from Herodotus via Mandeville) and the Amazon female warriors (Homer via many others) shows the tendency of Europeans like him to project on to the unknowns of America their own classical tropes.

Of course, this all helped to give Ralegh's book imaginative impact and resonance. Much is made also of the exemplary mission to protect the indigenous people from the cruel and grasping Spanish. The vision was of a grand alliance of England and the 'Empire of El Dorado', which would, if the Incas were trained in modern weapons, surely drive the Spanish from Peru. Indeed, Ralegh reports, an ancient Inca prophecy, discovered in their 'chiefest temple' in Peru, decreed that the Inca nation would be restored 'from Inglatierra'.

Yet alongside this heroic, noble purpose, and Ralegh's many words of praise for the welcoming local people, he often displays hard-headed pragmatism. He makes it clear that good treatment of the local population is as much about strategic good sense as kindness. He had learnt from his experiences of Virginia that it was vital for infant colonies to preserve good relations with indigenous inhabitants. They were more useful as allies. Notwithstanding this, he carefully notes their military backwardness and the apparent ease of dividing them against each other, which, he reminds the reader, was the key to the success of the conquests of Cortés and Pizarro. Of the golden city itself he wrote that if the putative King of El Dorado could not, as Ralegh predicted, 'be brought to tribute with great gladness . . . he hath neither shotte nor iron weapon in all his empire, and therefore may easily be conquered.'

In all, Ralegh's achievement in Guiana would prove to be more symbolic and literary than practical. But the book's contrasts between the fabulous and the mundane, and fantasy and reality, shaped English experience in the region for another 200 years. Certainly, Ralegh's shadow looms over everything that happened in Willoughbyland.

Four

THE HEIRS OF RALEGH

'All young gentlemen, soldiers and others
that live at home in idleness may here find
means to abandon and expel all their sloathful
humours and worthily exercise their spirits
in famous discoveries of many goodly
and rich territories.'

ROBERT HARCOURT, 1613

Ralegh's duties fighting the Spanish in European waters kept him occupied in the years following the publication of his book, but he continued to sponsor expeditions searching the rivers of Guiana for a way through into 'that upper rich country'. Interpreters continued to be carried back and forth between Guiana and his household in England.

Meanwhile, the international success of Ralegh's book had changed everything on the Wild Coast. El Dorado fever struck across Europe. Having been largely ignored, now the Guiana shoreline was at last mapped in detail by traders, explorers and gold-hunters from the United Provinces of the Netherlands and France as well as England. Soon, they would be followed by settlers, often with disastrous consequences.

Shortly after Keymis's departure from the coast, a Dutch expedition was, thanks to Ralegh's book, nosing up the Caroni following in his footsteps to the 'hill of silver' and the waterfall at the bottom of the river. They had been most impressed when off the coast they had encountered a canoeful of indigenous people – described by the Dutch as Caribs – who greeted them fondly with 'Anglees!' When the visitors turned out to be neither the returning Ralegh nor English at all, the Caribs didn't seem to mind. Anything was better than Spanish. The Dutch were shown 'much friendship' and told that a spirit, Wattopa, had foreseen their liberation by 'the Flamingos [Flemings] and Angleses'.

Of the mines described in the book, they found nothing. Their guides told them of 'a place about 6 miles higher up where there ought to be some mines, but the water had inundated it very much, so that it was impossible for us to visit it.'

They did note the presence of the new Spanish fort at San Thomé, a cluster of wooden buildings surrounded by a high stockade. Here were stationed sixty horsemen and a hundred musketeers, a number with their families who had accompanied them from Spain. It sounds like the most miserable posting in the Empire. The nearest Europeans were hundreds of miles away and as the surrounding indigenous people were hostile, the Spanish lived in a state of constant siege, virtually unable to leave the fort.

Still, if the fort could be kept manned and supplied, it was in a highly strategic position, bestriding the Orinoco and Caroni. The door to El Dorado, as decided by Berrío and Vera, was firmly shut. Another way would have to be found, as Keymis had already discovered.

Along the coast at Cayenne, the expedition came across an English ship out of London exchanging manufactured items such as knives, nails, needles, beads, mirrors and axes for tobacco, resin, hammocks, dyes, cotton and sought-after woods such as snakewood. Then two Dutch ships arrived, on similar missions. The French, they noticed, were also trading in the area. Nevertheless, the expedition's report noted that the whole coast remained 'unconquered' from the Orinoco to the Amazon.

The Virginia plantations were not yet established, and it was boom time in the tobacco trade. Soon warehouses were erected on riverbanks, and 'factors' left behind to amass stock for collection. Thus tiny settlements were established, usually just a few wooden buildings, protected by a wooden palisade. They were often short-lived and always chronically vulnerable to attack from the local population. But as demand increased, the next step was for the settlers to clear ground and plant crops themselves. Such colonies would also, of course, provide bases for expeditions in the interior to search for gold.

The earliest English colonies were based on the Wiapoco river, south-east of Cayenne (now the border between French Guyane and Brazil). The Wiapoco rises 200 miles from the sea in the Guiana uplands, and plunges down a series of waterfalls and steep rapids before flowing for fifty miles across a wide alluvial plain. This therefore promised both rich farmland for cash crops as well as potential access to the golden city in the interior.

On 21 March 1604, Puritan Charles Leigh, on board the fifty-ton *Olive Plant* with forty-six men and boys, 'departed from Woolwich with the intention to discover and inhabit some part of the Countrie of Guiana'. He was a veteran navigator of North America, the West Indies and the Guiana coast. His backing came from aristocratic friends and his brothers Sir Oliph and Sir John Leigh, the latter a friend of Ralegh. After a short time unsuccessfully trading in the Amazon delta – where they were offered only maize and 'blue-headed parrots' – on 22 May the vessel arrived at the Wiapoco river. There they found much better provisions on offer – honey, pineapples, cassava, fish, chickens and hogs – and 'a people readie to give us the best entertainment they could'.

European contact, although small compared to elsewhere in the region, had, of course, radically altered the lives and politics of the local indigenous peoples. By the beginning of the seventeenth century, smaller groups had loosely coalesced into two affiliations, delineated by Europeans as 'Caribs' and 'Arawaks'. In general, the former were seen as more independent, warlike and, reports claimed, cannibal. The 'Arawaks' or 'Arawagoes' were, in contrast, 'the best humoured Indians of America being both very just and generous minded people'. Cooperation with Arawaks was always easier, although they too were capable of 'atrocities', as the English of Willoughbyland were to discover.

For now, the Arawaks living around the Wiapoco estuary were keen to recruit the newcomers to help them against their Carib enemies as well as Portuguese slavers mounting incursions from the Amazon. It helped that the arrivals were of Ralegh's nationality. (One of the settlers, John Wilson, reported that 'they often speak of Sir Walter Ralegh', and one came all the way from the Orinoco 'to enquire of us of him, saying he promised to have returned to them before that time.') The 'divers conferences' Leigh now had with the 'chief Indians' were also aided by the presence among them of two local men who had been shipped to England on one of the earlier Ralegh-sponsored expeditions and since returned. One of them had taken an English name, William; the other was called Pluainma. The 'chief Indians' were happy for the English colonists to start planting provisions and tobacco some forty miles from the river mouth. They provided food and even agreed that five Arawak hostages, including the son of a 'chief', whom they named Martin, could be sent to England to underwrite the friendship.

But the clearing of huge trees and the planting was punishingly hard work and thanks to soggy marshes it was one of the unhealthiest places in the region. Men attracted to the expedition by the promises of gold and El Dorado had little heart for the more mundane challenges of growing tobacco, flax or cotton. In the heat and damp, the men mutinied, being 'so much discontented that they cried to their Captaine, "Home, Home."'

Led by one Martin Pring, a large faction declared it would rather go roving 'for spoyle and purchase' in the West Indies, than cut down the daunting jungle. The mutineers deliberately exhausted the group's provisions, so the Englishmen were forced to move back to the Arawak settlement at the river mouth; nonetheless, Leigh persuaded them 'to stay one whole year, through all extremities'. Another blow came with the arrival of a Dutch ship. The Hollanders paid high prices for the cotton wanted by the English, as well as sowing discord among the local people.

Leigh had, however, made a bargain that his men could occupy half a dozen huts in the village and be issued with provisions in return for mutual assistance against the Caribs. Ten of the weaker and more truculent English settlers were sent home, along with the five Arawak hostages, and a letter to Leigh's brother Sir Oliph Leigh. In it, Leigh stressed the opportunity to bring 'this simple hearted people to the knowledge of Christ', and that cotton and flax would yield a rich profit. 'I pray you Sir send me more weavers,' he wrote.

Leigh went on to complain about his 'mutinors and monstrous sailors' and requested he be sent a hundred men – gardeners and carpenters – provisions and tools, arms, three or four cannons, and two ships, one to return with trading goods, the other to guard the river mouth.

Soon afterwards came a raid on the river by Caribs from Cayenne. They had a nasty surprise when twenty-four Englishmen, in canoes paddled by their Arawak allies, shot out to meet them, with trumpets blowing. The muskets of the English soon had the Caribs on the retreat.

Once affairs were seemingly settled, Leigh, with William as interpreter, took a small group of men upriver, hiking above the falls to the high plateau above. Here he found more indigenous people willing to trade, but his other purpose, to find gold, was not successful. When he returned he found most of his men sick. Many had feet infested with worms, and the air was so damp, they complained, that they had to keep fires burning near their hammocks all night. Also, as Leigh reported, the 'Indians were not so kind to us as they had promised'. Soon after, a plot organised by the interpreter William to massacre the English visitors was only foiled when betrayed by the wives of those locals sent away as hostages and 'Martin's kindred'. A relief ship from home, with trade goods, provisions and thirty craftsmen, arrived soon after to find a quarter of the English settlers dead and Leigh himself 'very weak and much changed'.

Leigh sent the new men up the Cayenne and other nearby rivers, hoping that, unlike the Wiapoco, they might be gold-bearing, but by now Leigh was seriously ill with some sort of fever. He was loaded on to the ship to be taken home, but died on 20 March 1605. His death was kept from the colonists in case it caused a general abandonment.

More supplies and colonists were dispatched from England on 12 April 1605, but on arriving at the Wild Coast the vessel allowed itself to be carried to leeward. For weeks the crew tried to beat back to the Wiapoco against wind and currents, but then, with victuals exhausted, bore away to the Antilles, where most were massacred by the indigenous people of St Lucia. Before the end of the year, the English settlement was abandoned, with the survivors making their way home on French and Dutch ships. It was far from an auspicious start to English colonisation in the region.

Notwithstanding this failure, French and Dutch settlements were briefly established on the Wiapoco over the next couple of years, lured by the region's promised gold, rich trade, fertile soil and its position outside Spanish and Portuguese control. In 1609, an Englishman, Robert Harcourt, arrived with three ships and nearly a hundred eager settlers. He also had on board Martin, the chief's son sent back to England by Charles Leigh five years earlier, and Anthony Canabre, who had spent fourteen years in England living in Ralegh's household, having been shipped from the Orinoco area by Whiddon in 1594. Canabre had converted to Christianity and wore European clothes.

Harcourt came bearing a royal patent from James I, ordering him to claim in his name all the land 'lying betwixt the Rivers Amazon and Orinoco'. The death of Queen Elizabeth in March 1603 had threatened to rein in English activity in the Guianas. The new King took no pleasure in territorial expansion. But James's son, Prince Henry, was fascinated by Ralegh and Guiana, and had lent his support to Harcourt.

As Harcourt's three vessels – the eighty-ton *Rose* together with a smaller pinnace and sloop – approached the mouth of the Wiapoco, they were met by 'Indians . . . in two or three canoes, as well to learn of what Nation we were, as also to trade with us'. Once it was established the visitors were English, the men were happy to come on board and, in exchange for 'knives, beads, and such toys', supply the sailors with fish, pineapples, potatoes and cassava bread 'which were heartily welcome to my hungry company'.

Then Harcourt produced Martin, and the 'Indians . . . expressed much joy and contentment' having 'supposed he had been long dead'. Soon the local leaders were assembled on Harcourt's ship, bringing with them 'one who could speak English well'. It was John Provost, who had served as Keymis's interpreter a decade earlier. (Provost died soon after Harcourt's arrival. On the point of death he asked the English to sing a psalm for him, acknowledging that he was 'a wicked sinner', but 'that he died a Christian, yea a Christian of England'.)

With bilingual people in both parties, negotiations went well. Harcourt started by bringing 'to their remembrance the exploits of Sir Walter Ralegh'. He then promised them help against their local enemies. In return he was offered provisions and accommodation. Harcourt, for his part, found his hosts 'a loving, tractable, and gentle people, affecting and preferring the English before all nations whatsoever'.

As with Leigh's expedition, the English moved inland to plant tobacco. The soil, Harcourt reported, was 'exceeding rich, never yet broken up . . . but still remains in the greatest perfection of fertility'. He planned that 'by planting vines, we shall make good store of sack, and Canary wine, which in those parts are needful, and very wholesome, and will greatly comfort and lighten the hearts of our countrymen and make them jovial.' But with the coming of the drier season, his attention turned elsewhere as he led his men further inland 'in search of those Golden Mountains, promised unto us before the beginning of our voyage'. Turning up nothing, the men became dispirited, and only with great difficulty did Harcourt suppress a mutiny.

The city of Manoa, or El Dorado, fully imagined in an engraving from 1599, which also shows Europeans in the act of discovery, having carried their boats from the headwaters of the (real) River Essequibo.

Leaving his brother in charge with about thirty men, Harcourt now set sail for England to raise new recruits and money for his colony. Coasting westwards, he landed four or five men at the Cayenne river, and another small group led by his cousin Unton Fisher at the Maroni river, with instructions to get to the truth about El Dorado. Fisher gallantly fought his way 300 miles upriver, but was forced to turn back through lack of provisions and shortly afterwards drowned.

Back in England, Harcourt published a prospectus to attract new settlers and capital – 'We may by the gracious assistance of our Good God, gain unto our sovereign the dominion of a rich and mighty empire' – but the death of Prince Henry in 1612 had robbed him of influential support. Meanwhile on the Wiapoco, fever had wiped out most of the remaining settlers. Lacking support from distant England, by 1614 it was abandoned, with the few bedraggled survivors eventually reaching other European outposts nearby. So it was another failure for the English colonisation of Guiana.

French settlement efforts, marked by extreme persistence and recurring disaster, had been concentrated around the Cayenne river. The first wave of colonists, arriving in 1613, unwisely picked a fight with local people and all were killed. The second wave, in 1635, suffered the same fate, while the third, of 400 men eight years later, started well under the leadership of Charles Poncet de Brétigny. But de Brétigny, as one historian has written, was 'more fit to have been confined in a mad house than to govern a colony'. Learning nothing from previous efforts, he quarrelled with the local indigenous people, who, of course, retaliated; then he started persecuting his own colonists. He seems to have taken a great interest in torture, and used any excuse to try out inventions of his own. When he ran out of criminals, he demanded that people tell him their dreams, and punished them if the mood took him. One man who had dreamt that the governor had died was broken on the wheel.

Eventually the majority of the surviving colonists fled this tyrant, preferring to risk it in the jungle inland. When de Brétigny pursued them with the few men still loyal to him, they were all ambushed by indigenous people and killed. Some of the French colonists then left for St Kitts, while others staggered on for another two years.

The Dutch also had their share of disasters, with attempted colonies on the Amazon wiped out by the Portuguese and their local allies, but they were more successful to the west, by 1615 establishing a well-guarded settlement on the Essequibo river, and reinforcing their Pomeroon outpost. From here they traded iron and metal tools for tobacco, cloth and dyes, which became a Dutch speciality. On other rivers, trading posts were set up far inland, and good relations established with locals. The Dutch were fast becoming Europe's leading economic power, with an unrivalled merchant-marine and trade networks across America and the East. After the English failures on the Wiapoco, it now looked as though Ralegh's 'Beautiful Empire of Guiana' would fall to them, rather than the English. Then, in 1617, Ralegh himself returned to the Wild Coast.

Five

RALEGH'S LAST VOYAGE

'Fallen from his high estate,
And welt'ring in his blood:
Deserted at his utmost need
By those his former bounty fed.'

JOHN DRYDEN, 'ALEXANDER'S FEAST', 1697

Sir Walter Ralegh had fallen foul of the machinations, plotting and jockeying for position that had accompanied the arrival of the new King James Stuart after Queen Elizabeth's death. He found himself accused of involvement in a plot, paid for with Spanish money, to replace James with his cousin Arbella Stuart. Much of the trial's records have been lost, so it is unclear if Ralegh was guilty – the claims may have been based on nothing more than overheard treasonous conversations. His family would later say that he had infiltrated the plot and was preparing to reveal all to the King. If this was his defence, it failed and he was convicted of treason, a capital crime. The King, however, commuted the sentence to life imprisonment, which perhaps suggests he was unsure of the verdict. Nevertheless, from July 1603 Ralegh was confined in the Tower of London.

There, he had a small botanical garden and some chemistry equipment with which he practised extracting gold from ore gathered on his Guiana trip. He wrote a number of treatises, as well as an epic *History of the World*. But Guiana remained his obsession. Lawrence Keymis was a frequent visitor and Ralegh continued to support expeditions, including a contribution of £600 to Sir Thomas Roe, who in 1610 explored the Amazon as well as the rivers of the Wild Coast. Roe returned with the conclusion that there was no El Dorado, stories of which, he said, 'I found by experience false', but he also reported that the fort at San Thomé, close to the mines identified by Ralegh and Keymis, although rich from trade in tobacco and hides, was extremely weak, with a mutinous garrison. It might, he suggested, be captured without a shot being fired.

Already Ralegh had been petitioning the King, the Queen consort, the council and individual courtiers for permission to sail to Guiana to locate the fabled mines. He was released at last on 19 March 1616 to find the gold, on the condition – on pain of death – that he did not inflict any injury on subjects of the King of Spain.

James was desperately short of money and knew that public opinion was strongly in favour of Ralegh's quest, but his motives for allowing the expedition to sail were complicated. Having married his daughter Princess Elizabeth to Frederick V of the Palatinate in 1613, and thus shored up links to German Protestantism, James looked to balance this with a countering marriage of his son into the Spanish royal family. This caused alarm with the rising anti-Spanish faction within the English court's Privy Council, who supported Ralegh's project in the hope that it would provoke war with Spain. James for his part wanted to use it to prod the Spanish into the dynastic alliance, aware that he could wash his hands of Ralegh if it so suited him.

It was hard to see how Ralegh might win. There were three possible outcomes: that he would have gold for the King and no conflict with the Spanish; that he would have gold, but at the cost of blood; or that there would be Spanish casualties, and nothing to show for it. The first was highly improbable: the idea of Englishmen digging a mine almost within sight of the fort at San Thomé was a nonsense; recent years had seen an escalation of efforts by the Spanish to defend their settlements from incursions by other Europeans. The second was effectively Ralegh's gamble: that the King would be swayed by the treasure despite his aversion of war with Spain. For the last outcome, Ralegh knew he would just have to throw himself at the King's mercy.

Ralegh had everything to lose, James nothing. By expressly forbidding what looked like an almost inevitable military clash, the King had covered himself; Ralegh could be hung out to dry in an instant. James further distanced himself by omitting the customary words 'trusty and well-beloved' from the commission issued to Ralegh. This was in case they could be interpreted as a pardon for Ralegh's 1603 treason conviction. It was better to have the death sentence hanging over his champion. Furthermore, James handed over to the Spanish ambassador Count Gondomar details of Ralegh's fleet as well as his proposed route.

Ralegh raised the huge sum of £30,000 and assembled a large and powerful force, fourteen ships in all, and some thousand men, which left Plymouth in June 1617. It quickly became apparent, however, that the rank and file was of questionable quality. Ralegh himself described them as 'the scum of men', forever brawling and complaining. Part of their discontent was at the endless delays and forced inactivity, as storms drove the fleet back to Plymouth, then into Falmouth, then Kinsale in Ireland. One of the smaller vessels sank and a larger ship was forced into Bristol.

The Canaries were not reached until 6 September. They took on provisions and fresh water at Gomera, but soon after they left sickness broke out, with one ship alone having fifty men unfit for duty. To get fresh meat, the fleet headed for the Cape Verde islands; there a hurricane fell on them, sinking another of the smaller vessels and driving the rest of the ships out to sea, where they were then becalmed.

Forty-two died on board the flagship, including one of the chief refiners and assayers for the mine. Ralegh himself developed a fever and was unable to eat for several days.

On 11 November the fleet finally arrived off the Wiapoco, before heading into the mouth of the Cayenne. Ralegh's spirits rose when he was welcomed as the returning deliverer of the indigenous peoples from the cruel Spaniards. He wrote to his wife, 'To tell you that I might be here King of the Indians were a vanitie; but my name hath lived among them.' In Ralegh's view, this enthusiasm meant that the area had been voluntarily ceded to England by its native possessors. All he needed was some gold to entice his Sovereign to enter into his inheritance.

So the fleet sailed on to the Orinoco. Ralegh was still sick, so he put his old and trusted friend Lawrence Keymis in charge of the force that would head upriver. This consisted of the five remaining ships of shallow enough draught, loaded with 150 sailors and 250 troops, along with provisions for a month. Included in the party was Walter, known as Wat, Ralegh's twenty-one-year-old son.

Two vessels immediately ran aground and were left behind. Then, fighting against a strong current, it took the remaining boats three weeks to reach San Thomé. It seems that the intention was to lay siege to the town by water and land, in order to bottle up the Spanish troops while the English miners did their work. Nevertheless, it was hoped that a show of force would itself be enough for the reportedly rebellious faction inside to betray the town to Ralegh's men without a shot being fired.

English soldiers were landed three miles downriver from the town, while the larger of the vessels sailed on until they were opposite the fort, where they anchored. They came under fire from mortars inside the defences, but did not respond. Meanwhile, the landing party marched in battle order to the town. But just half a mile away they were ambushed by a small group of Spaniards. A battle was underway, whatever the intentions of the English might have been. There followed a running fight back to the fort. Before anyone drew breath, Wat Ralegh, in what was later described as 'unadvised daringness', led a storm of its walls.

It was soon over, and the defences were in English hands. There had only been thirty-six Spanish soldiers, of whom three were killed; the rest fled into the bush. On the English side only two men were killed. One of these, however, his throat ripped out by a musket ball, was Wat Ralegh.

For nearly a month, the English held the town. But parties going beyond its walls looking for gold samples or the rumoured mines were frequently ambushed by the surviving Spanish. Keymis now lost his nerve, and control of his men. Terrified that Spanish reinforcements might come upriver and cut him off, he ordered the town to be burnt and his men to sail back downstream to the sea.

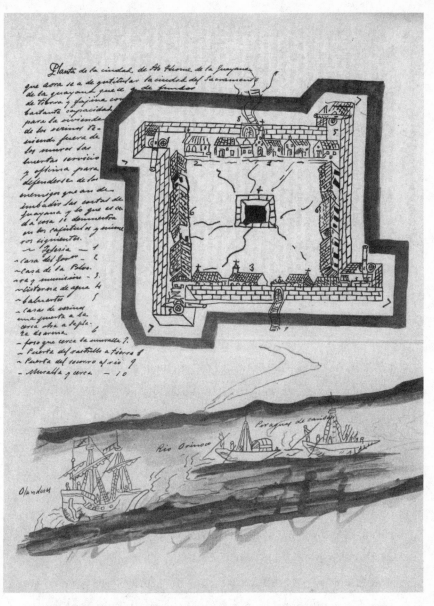

A Spanish sketch of San Thomé made at the time of the disastrous English attack. Elements of Ralegh's force can be seen on the river.

Keymis returned to Trinidad to face his captain. Ralegh had already heard about the death of his son. He now refused to accept Keymis's apology for the loss and for his failure to gather any but a handful of rock samples. Keymis asked if that was Ralegh's 'resolution; I told him it was,' Ralegh later reported. 'He then replied in these words, "I know then, Sir, what course to take," and went out of my cabin up into his own, into which he was no sooner entered but I heard a pistol go off.' Keymis had blown a hole in his chest, and when this failed to kill him, he placed the tip of a dagger under his breastbone and drove it upwards into his heart.

Ralegh knew that his own life was now forfeit and he resolved to go back up the Orinoco himself. 'Seeing my son was lost,' he wrote, 'I cared not if he had lost a hundred more in opening the mine, so my credit had been saved . . . I would have left my body at San Thomé by my son's.' But his sickly and demoralised men would not follow him. Desertions came thick and fast, and several captains slipped off with their ships, bent on piracy. Soon the fleet had melted away.

Ralegh abandoned the Orinoco and sailed to St Kitts. From there, on 22 March, he wrote to his wife with news of the death of their son. 'My brains are broken and 'tis a torment for me to write . . . The Lord blesse you and Comfort you, that you may bear patiently the death of your valiant son. God knows, I never knew what sorrow meant till now . . . Comfort your heart (dear Bess), I shall sorrow for us both; and I shall sorrow the less because I have not long to sorrow, because not long to live.'

Ralegh's ship, depleted of crew, limped into Plymouth harbour on 21 June 1618, almost exactly a year after his departure. Those who had returned first had already been seen by the King, and had suggested that Ralegh had invented the mine in order to enrich himself by piracy and that he planned to defect to the French. Debating the issue of Ralegh's fate, the pro-Spanish party won the day with the King, who then offered to send the newly returned Ralegh to Madrid for execution. The Spanish were happy for him to do the job.

Ralegh was executed on 29 October, having shown complete composure as he delivered a forty-five-minute oration from the scaffold in which he denied all the accusations against him, blaming 'a base Frenchman' for spreading lies.

To a report that he had only gone to Guiana to secure his freedom, he countered, 'It was my full intent to go for gold, for the benefit of his Majesty and the rest of my countrymen.' He ended with a prayer 'to the great God of heaven, who I have grievously offended, being a man full of all vanity, and have lived a sinful life in all sinful callings, having been a soldier, a captain, and sea-captain, and a courtier, which are all places of wickedness and vice; that God, I say, would forgive me . . . So I take my leave of you all.' The execution brought more odium from the general population upon James than any other act of his reign. From among the crowd at the scaffold came a loud shout: 'We have not such another head to be struck off.'

Despite the ruin and death of Guiana's most famous and influential promoter, the hope of establishing an English settlement on the Wild Coast lived on among his protégés, one of whom, Captain Roger North, in 1620 successfully petitioned to take over Harcourt's grant from the King. Funded by a coterie of aristocrats, North and a small party of settlers established an outpost 100 miles up the Wiapoco, joined by the ragged survivors of Harcourt's colony. There, 'the site of the country and people so contented them, that never men thought themselves more happie,' as one settler reported. But after complaints from the Spanish ambassador, North was recalled and thrown in the Tower. A handful of his men struggled on, but most left to establish England's first Caribbean island settlement on St Kitts. Thus, as an afterthought from Guiana, the English empire in the West Indies was founded.

The accession of Charles I in 1625 saw a change in policy and an encouragement of blatant challenges to the power of Spain in the Americas. All three upstart powers – England, France, the United Provinces – now handed out charters for possession of the whole of the Wild Coast. The English claim was based on the explorations and treaties of Ralegh, Leigh, Harcourt and Roe. In January 1627 four ships sailed again for the Wiapoco (possibly with Harcourt on board), but the new colony was soon abandoned, bringing to an end more than twenty years of struggle on the river. Other English settlements on the Amazon were destroyed by the Portuguese or simply withered away. Internal conflict, disease, desertion and hunger were common causes for the failures; most frequent, though, was attack by indigenous people armed with poison-tipped arrows. A contemporary described the agonising end this caused: 'sometimes dying stark mad, sometimes their bowels breaking out of their bodies: which are presently discoloured as black as pitch, and so unsavoury, as no man can endure to cure, or to attend them.'

So what of the Suriname river, soon to become the site of Willoughbyland? Ralegh had described the 'river of Surenama' as 'the best part of all that tract of land between the Rivers of Amazones and Orienoque'. According to a notarial deed from 1617, concerning the murder of an indigenous man and a retaliatory attack, the Dutch were there first. In 1613, two merchants, Dirck Claesz van Sanen and Nicolaas Baliestel, entered the river mouth and headed upstream. It didn't look promising as the riverbanks were muddy and marshy, a stinking bog. But about fifteen miles from the sea, the ground rose a little, and millennia of shellfish, feeding on the ooze of the river bed, had deposited enough shells which when compacted had formed rock of a sort. Here, on the right bank, was an indigenous village called Purmerbo.

The Dutchmen landed, and in the way of things formed a friendship based on gifts and trade of axes, knives and trinkets. Soon they had established a warehouse and a group of smaller buildings, all of wood, protected by a palisade of sharpened tree trunks on the site of what would later become Fort Willoughby (now Fort Zeelandia). The operation continued for at least three or four years, but after that seems to have closed down.

According to scattered references, there were also brief French occupations of the river. The first English Willoughbylanders supposedly found the ruins of a French fort and in an account from the 1660s there is a mention of Frenchmen being 'cut off' in Suriname before the English came. It seems that in 1639 a French colony, originally of 370 men, settled on the Saramacca river, just west of the Suriname. The following year, 'many families' came from France. 'They lived peaceably until the year 1642,' one usually accurate source maintains, by which time they had 'great supplies of men, ammunition and provisions from France. They grew careless, spread themselves to Suriname and Corentyne, had difference with the Indians, and were all cut off in one Day.' Another account suggests that the French fort was instead built by an expedition – possibly a breakaway group – from Cayenne during the short-lived de Brétigny colony, which perished in 1645.

There are also sketchy Jewish records of settlement in Suriname that go back to 1639, and more reliable evidence from the 1640s. After attacks by the aggressive Dutch West India Company culminating in 1630, the Dutch had controlled large parts of Brazil, and provided a safe haven from the Inquisition for Jews and Conversos. But in the early 1640s the Portuguese planters launched a series of rebellions that progressively drove out the Dutch. With the spectre of the Inquisition looming over them, many of the colony's Jewish inhabitants moved north to the Guianas, with at least some establishing themselves upriver on the Suriname, in the area still known today as Jewish Savannah or Joden Savanne.

An illustration of Jewish Savannah in the early eighteenth century. At one time it was home to more than a quarter of the colony's white population.

Further upriver is a small town now called Marchallkreek. This is named after the leader of an English colony that was established there sometime in the 1630s or 1640s. Captain Marshall seems to have come from Barbados with sixty English colonists and a view to growing tobacco. They may have come from Tobago after the failure of a similar venture there, thanks to 'want of supplies' and the hostility of the local 'Carribees'. By 1643 it was, reportedly, 'a flourishing community of three hundred English families'. But two years later, it all came to an end when 'they espoused the quarrel of the French and were cut off by the natives.'

Francis Willoughby would have known about these unfortunate precedents for English colonialism in South America: how perilously difficult it was to survive, how the settlers had found, as one put it, 'little other welcome than a resting place for their bones', and the vital importance of effective leadership. Furthermore, the growing of tobacco for export, which had for a large part motivated the earlier efforts, was no longer so profitable. But he would not be deterred; by the time of the establishment of Willoughbyland in the early 1650s, there was a new imperative worth almost any risk: sugar, known as 'white gold'.

Six

FRANCIS LORD WILLOUGHBY

'Since all is gone at home, it is time to
provide elsewhere for a being.'

FRANCIS WILLOUGHBY FROM BARBADOS

TO HIS WIFE, 1651

Francis Willoughby would be described by contemporaries as both charming and self-centred; his military and political careers would show him to be at times impetuous and at others indecisive. In many ways he was a visionary, but he was also an inveterate plotter and schemer.

He was born around 1603 into a wealthy landed Lincolnshire family, inheriting the title Baron Willoughby of Parham while still a child. In 1628 he married well, to Elizabeth Cecil from one of the country's richest dynasties, but perhaps more important to his future were his wife's mother's family, the Noells, who were amongst the most important financial backers of English exploits in the Caribbean. Thus Willoughby moved in circles more aware than most of the potential riches of the West Indies colonies.

Francis Lord Willoughby, 5th Baron Parham, leading his men fighting for Parliament in the Civil War.

During the 1630s, Willoughby's relationship with the Crown soured. Like many, he objected to Charles I's efforts to rule – and raise revenue – without recourse to Parliament. As a Presbyterian, he opposed the King's attempts in 1639 to impose episcopal church government on Scotland, and the following year was amongst a group of aristocratic signers of a petition to the King to recall Parliament and to listen to its grievances.

Charles bowed to pressure, but relations with the new Parliament deteriorated to the point of war. Willoughby had been made a lord lieutenant of part of Lincolnshire, and in that capacity in March 1642 he was ordered separately by both the King and Parliament to raise local troops to fight their causes. He chose to obey the latter, although he wrote an apologetic letter to the King.

From the autumn he was colonel of a regiment of Horse under the Parliamentary general the Earl of Essex, and in January 1643 became commander-in-chief of Lincolnshire Parliamentary forces. As a military leader his achievements were modest at best. In July he captured Gainsborough but then lost it, followed by Lincoln. Willoughby was demoted, placed under the Earl of Manchester. A success at Bolingbroke Castle in November was then followed by involvement in a disaster for Parliament at Newark, where a Roundhead army led by Sir John Meldrum was outmanoeuvred and forced to surrender to a Royalist army half its size. The fallout included the accusation that Willoughby's men had refused to obey Meldrum's orders.

Indeed, Willoughby had gained a reputation for bickering with his fellow officers. He would shortly be forced to apologise in the House of Lords for quarrelling with the Earl of Manchester. Cromwell, on the other hand, linked Willoughby's military failures with the licence he allowed his men, complaining of 'ungodly officers', one of whom had supposedly ordered a constable 'to bring him in some wenches'.

Willoughby turned his energies to politics, leading the Presbyterian faction within Parliament and opposing the growing power of the army. He was a moderate, distrustful of the levelling principles taking hold of radical MPs and in the ranks: in 1644 he warned, 'We are all hasting to an early ruin. Nobility and gentry are going down apace.' This put him at loggerheads with the increasing sway in Parliament of 'fiercer spirits'. His brother-in-law Bulstrode Whitelocke warned that Willoughby was 'in danger of his fortune, honour, and life, upon a new faction rising up, and all his former merits forgotten.'

Nevertheless, Willoughby was elected leader of the House of Lords in August 1647; but in the meantime he had been making arrangements to cover all eventualities, reorganising his assets and moving property to trustees. Most importantly, he took measures to move money, and if necessary himself, out of the country altogether. Perhaps on the advice of his Noell in-laws, it was to the West Indies that he looked for a refuge.

Following the settlement of St Kitts in 1623 by survivors of the failed Guiana colony of Roger North, two years later an English vessel, returning from the Guiana coast but blown off course, anchored at Barbados and claimed the island for King James. In 1627, the first colonisers landed. Ten years later there were more than 10,000 inhabitants, while

English and Irish settlers from St Kitts, many of them former indentured servants, had spread out to the islands of Nevis, Montserrat and Antigua.

Before the mid-1640s, colonists in Barbados had produced tobacco, cotton, indigo and ginger and struggled to make it pay. Few ships came to its port at Bridgetown and many inhabitants went hungry. But then the leading planters started an experiment to grow and process sugar cane. This was immensely difficult, but after many early problems, and with help from the Dutch who were growing sugar in Brazil, it was mastered. On the London market the sugar fetched four times the price of any of the other crops. In next to no time, almost the entire island was covered in sugar plantations, and the capital Bridgetown became one of America's busiest ports. From a failing backwater, Barbados had become 'one of the richest spots of earth under the sun'.

The 'Charibee Islands' were under the government of a proprietor, a position akin to that of a feudal lord. The proprietor appointed local governors, and in return for tenancy on the land, the planters paid the proprietor rents, custom duties or a simple poll tax. James I had given this position to his court favourite James Hay, 1st Earl of Carlisle. But Carlisle was famously spendthrift, and when he died in

OVERLEAF: *A map of Barbados published in 1657. Here the 'Sugar Revolution' occurred, which would radically change English colonialism in the Caribbean.*

A Scale of five Miles

A topographicall Description and Admeasurement of the YLAND of BARBADOS in the West INDYAES with the Mrs. Names of the Seuerall plantacons

The tenn Thousande Acres of Lande which Belongeth to the Merchants of London.

1636, he left behind a mountain of debt for his successor the 2nd Earl, also named James Hay.

While in 1643 the planters in Barbados used the chaos of the Civil War quietly to stop paying proprietorial dues, angry creditors closed in on the 2nd Earl, eventually appealing successfully to the Commons for redress for the £11,000 they were owed. To meet this debt, Carlisle had no option but to mortgage the proprietorship.

Thus, in February 1647, he came to an agreement with Francis Willoughby to lease him the islands for twenty-one years, sharing between them what revenue he could raise. He also gave Willoughby a patent constituting him 'Lieutenant-General of the Charibbee Islands, for the better settling and securing them', and promised to have this confirmed by the King, which was duly achieved.

Willoughby's insurance policy would soon be needed. September 1647 saw the internal struggle in Parliament between the radical Independents and the moderate Presbyterians won by the former, thanks to help from the army. Now moderates like Willoughby, who wanted Parliament to compromise with the King, were regarded as traitors. Willoughby was one of seven lords impeached and thrown into the Tower. For four months they remained imprisoned without charge, until protests saw their release in January on a bail of £4,000 each. The following month the Commons issued the charge of treason against them.

Willoughby jumped bail, fled to join exiled Royalists in Holland and openly joined their side.

The following year, Willoughby was appointed vice admiral of a small fleet that had recently, in sympathy with protests in Wales and Kent against army rule, gone over to the King's side, 'though he had never been at sea or was at all known to the seamen'. It appears his talents as a naval commander were on a par with his performance on land, and he was replaced before the end of the year.

As punishment for his Royalist activities, Willoughby's English estates were sequestered by Parliament at the end of 1649. A few weeks later, having secured protectors for his wife and children, he set sail for Barbados. From there he wrote to his wife, 'Since all is gone at home, it is time to provide elsewhere for a being.'

In fact, Willoughby was following a path well-trodden by fellow Royalist refugees. As their cause had failed at home, many Cavaliers had gathered what capital they could and made for the West Indies. Humphrey Walrond was typical: captured after the surrender of the Royalist enclave of Bridgwater in July 1645, he was released only on condition of paying a huge fine. Instead, he sold up his estates in England and together with his brothers Edward and George fled to Barbados. The following year, Thomas Modyford, after the fall of Exeter to Parliamentary forces under Sir Thomas Fairfax, decided he too was 'willing to shift', and sailed for Barbados with a large household. In all, by the end of 1648, the Caribbean was awash with exiled Cavaliers.

For a long time in Barbados an agreement stood to carry on with business and not to mention the conflict at home. In fact, if anyone did, they were compelled to provide a roast turkey dinner for anyone in hearing. By the late 1640s, there were recognisable groups of Roundheads and Royalists, but friendships and marriages crossed the divide and the colony remained effectively neutral, tolerant of religious differences and enjoying a lack of interference from home as the Civil War dragged on. Both sides in England petitioned the Carlisle-appointed governor Philip Bell, but he played them off against each other, declaring, 'against the king we are resolved never to be, and without the friendship of the parliament and free trade of London ships we are not able to subsist.'

But news of the execution of the King in January 1649 was too much for Royalists such as the Walrond brothers, who had been busy taking a firm grip on the island's Assembly and Council. In mid-1649 they had the island's treasurer arrested on trumped-up charges and replaced with their own protégé. William Byam, from a Somerset family that had relocated to Ireland, had been captured with Humphrey Walrond at Bridgwater. A fervent monarchist, he was described by his enemies as a 'known malignant'. His new duties as treasurer in Barbados included responsibility for the island's arsenal and defence.

While the Royalists plotted to have the island declare for the King, a bitter pamphlet war broke out, with each side making serious threats and accusing the other of preparing a coup d'état. Attempts at conciliation by the moderate Thomas Modyford got nowhere. The Royalists were now openly arming themselves, and soon a well-mounted troop was at large in Humphrey Walrond's parish of St Philip. The brash young Cavaliers rode about swearing to slaughter all 'the Independent doggs' who refused to 'drink to the Figure II' (Charles II).

In late April 1650, governor Philip Bell issued an edict threatening capital punishment on anyone who took up arms, but it was too late. The next day, having invented an 'Independent' plot to seize control of the island, Humphrey Walrond marched on Bridgetown at the head of a powerful armed force. The governor had no option but to accede to his demands: complete Cavalier control of the arsenal and the body of the governor himself; the disarmament and punishment of the Roundheads; and a declaration of loyalty to Charles II. The last was publicly made on 3 May. Roundheads on the island were fined, banished, and in a few cases literally branded as traitors (the letter 'T' burnt on to their faces). It could have been worse: an extremist faction led by William Byam had urged the summary execution of the 'Independent dogges'. Nonetheless, deep, long-lasting animosities were created that would have a huge impact on events in Willoughbyland.

So when Francis Willoughby arrived as the new governor he found the island in turmoil and his own position uncertain. As a representative of the King, he was unwanted by the remaining Roundhead faction, and he was mistrusted as a turncoat by the Royalists. Humphrey Walrond warned that 'he was once a Roundhead, and might be again'. But Willoughby handled the delicate situation with great charm, tact and intelligence. He restated the oath of loyalty to Charles Stuart as Charles II, laying on a lavish celebration at his own expense, 'the trumpeters receiving money and as much wine as they could drink', as was reported to London. But he also reversed the sentences of banishment on the leading Roundhead planters and isolated and then removed from all public office the extremist Humphrey Walrond. Such 'politic conduct', it was even said, saw Willoughby 'welcomed as a blessing from God'.

Having settled tempers on the island, Willoughby's next move was to try to rebuild bridges with London. In the hope of coming to an arrangement with Parliament, he sent a local planter, George Marten, to London to start negotiations, and to bring back the formerly banished Roundhead planters. Marten, like William Byam, would feature prominently in the Willoughbyland story. He was no doubt chosen because of his elder brother Henry, who was a Parliamentary spymaster, member of the Council of

State, and a hard-line anti-Royalist who had always urged strong action against the King. Henry Marten had been one of the first to write tracts denying the King's infallibility and during the second part of the Civil War he had raised a Leveller-dominated regiment, whose watchwords were 'For the People's freedom against all tyrants whatsoever'. He had been a leading regicide, and together with Oliver Cromwell had organised others to sign the King's death warrant.

The King had referred to him as 'an ugly rascal' and a 'whore-monger'. John Aubrey described him as 'a great lover of pretty girls to whom he was so liberal that he spent the greatest part of his estate' upon them. Much of the rest of his money went on wine. All of this would contribute to his falling out with Cromwell. When he dissolved the Long Parliament in 1653, he would declare Henry Marten a member 'whose immorality is a disgrace to the house'.

George, who was born around 1608, shared Henry's weakness for women and wine and was constantly in debt. During the Civil War he had played a key part in the naval coup that installed the Earl of Warwick as admiral, and captained the family bark, the *Marten*, in the Parliamentary navy. It seems that 1644 saw George working as a Parliamentary spy in France. Then, two years later, in a bid to rebuild the family fortune, he sailed for Barbados, where he bought land and started growing tobacco.

Willoughby's instructions to Marten were 'to prevent all misunderstanding and to settle a perfect and free trade with them'. In effect this meant offering pretty much anything in return for being allowed to do business in Barbados with the Dutch and to keep Willoughby in his position.

It was a dangerous mission. As the representative of a traitor, Marten could have found himself hanged. But in the event, on his arrival in London he struggled to find anyone to see him. When he finally got access to the corridors of power, no one wanted to hear that the Barbadians 'looked on themselves as a free people'. Because of the powerful lobby of English merchants interested in the Barbados trade, there could be no question of the commercial freedom that Willoughby desired. Instead Parliament declared the Barbadians to be 'notorious robbers and traitors', imposed a trade embargo and started readying a force under Admiral Sir George Ayscue to subdue the island. George Marten then prudently added his name to a petition calling on Barbados 'to renounce all obedience to Charles Stuart, and acknowledge the supreme authority of the present Parliament.'

Willoughby heard about the failure of Marten's mission in February 1651 and, hoping the Royalist cause to be far from lost, determined on resistance in spite of the contrary advice of his wife in England, writing to her, 'If ever they get this island, it shall cost them more than it is worth before they have it.' He bought in weapons and ammunition from Dutch and New England traders, but his hopes rested on action by Charles II to recover his kingdom and, nearer to West Indian waters, on a Royalist fleet under the King's cousin Prince Rupert, which was still at large in the Atlantic.

Yet however heroic Willoughby might have sounded when writing to his wife, he was shrewd enough to realise he needed a fallback plan. In fact, within a couple of months of his arrival in Barbados, he had sent a ship with forty men to explore the Suriname river, only two or three days' sailing from Barbados. Willoughby, possibly backed by his in-laws the Noell family as well as other colonial financiers, had provided the vessel and 'the loan of a parcel of Indian trade'.

Suriname represented not only a 'last refuge', but also a stunning opportunity. Willoughby could quickly see that Barbados had a surplus population ready to take on a new challenge. Smaller landowners had been squeezed out by the big sugar plantations and white workers replaced by enslaved Africans. He also would have taken on board concerns that Barbados was too dry and that its soil was being fast exhausted by the nutrient-hungry sugar plant. Suriname seemed to offer the answer: huge, empty of European settlers, wet and wildly fertile. English attempts at colonisation of Guiana, as we have seen, had all ended in failure. But if the land could be planted in cane, then the rewards would outweigh almost any dangers.

Willoughby was alive to other attractions, too. Suriname also offered profit in the 'Indian trade' in tobacco and cotton goods, as well as rare woods and dyestuffs. Best of all, it promised the possibility of gold, even El Dorado. In all, it appealed to Willoughby's vision of himself as a pioneer and architect of grandiose schemes, in which he saw himself as the successor to Sir Walter Ralegh.

In command of Willoughby's first reconnaissance mission to Suriname was Major Anthony Rous. He appears to have been closely connected with George Marten: they owned neighbouring plantations in Barbados. Marten six years later would describe him as 'my very kind and loyal friend a person of as much honesty and courtesy as I have ever met with in these parts'. Rous seems to have been a Caribbean jack of all trades, typical of this transitional time: a settler and planter in Barbados and Suriname (his name appears as the owner of an estate in Willoughbyland in 1667); a privateer sailing with Captain William Jackson on his buccaneering tour along the Spanish Main in 1642; a soldier fighting in Jamaica during Cromwell's invasion of 1655. There is a little bit of Ralegh in this contradictory make-up. An English account of the late 1660s describes him as 'a Gentleman of great Gallantrie and Prudence and of Long Experience in ye West Indies'.

His record as a military officer in Jamaica shows more enthusiasm than skill, but he was clearly a fine diplomat.

The indigenous people of the Suriname river had been described seven years before as the most dangerous of all on the Wild Coast, 'being man-eaters, and very false in performing their promises'. Certainly, European 'factories' and mini-settlements seem, from the meagre records, to have fared there even worse than on the other Guiana rivers. But Rous reported back that he had met 'divers' 'Caribs' and by 'reviving the name of Sir Walter Ralegh gave the English firm footing in those parts'. There had been a warm welcome, and all had declared a 'firme peace'.

For five months, the forty Englishmen mapped the shoals of the river mouth, traded with the local people and explored upriver, noting how the higher ground further from the sea promised better land for plantations and fewer mosquitoes than the swampy shoreline. The local game, called 'partridges' and 'pheasants' by the Englishmen, were easy prey for their unfamiliar muskets and they ate well and often. No one got ill, which was unusual for the West Indies anywhere. Instead, they reported 'the air to be so pure, and the water so good, as they had never such stomachs in their lives'.

Of the status of the 'Indian village' of Purmerbo there was no detail given, nor of the numbers, patterns of settlement and trade, or lives of the people then inhabiting what would become Willoughbyland. Ralegh on the Orinoco was much more thorough than his successors in this regard. But Rous did report that his party had found one solitary white settler,

Jacob Enoch, a Dutch Jew, living a little way upriver with his family. What we do know, however, is that Rous brought two 'Indian kings' back to Barbados to meet Willoughby. After talks and payment of some kind, they agreed to 'receive' the English to 'settle amongst them' in Suriname, as Willoughby wrote to his wife in August 1651.

While the Parliament force to subdue Barbados dithered in England and then at last set sail in August 1651, Willoughby sent Rous back to Suriname with a hundred men 'to take possession'. Work started on repairing the old French fort by the site of the local village of Purmerbo; trees were felled and huts built nearby. From then on, there was regular traffic: every week Willoughby's ships – one of twenty guns and two smaller vessels – ferried about fifty men, together with 'Warlike Furniture and Ammunition', provisions and tools across to Suriname. The ships returned with cotton, tobacco and hammocks acquired from the local people. Willoughby wrote to his wife that he hoped 'in a few years to have many thousands there'. He also sent some of his own household to claim estates in his name as Rous began allotting riverside plantations to the Barbadian settlers and London investors.

Back in Barbados, there was good news for the Royalists, it seemed: Prince Rupert's flotilla was on its way to the West Indies; a Dutch ship brought intelligence that Charles II was at the head of a victorious army only forty miles from

London, that the population had risen to support him, and that Cromwell was dead. On 15 October there were widespread celebrations across the island, with bonfires, dancing and feasting. Willoughby enjoyed himself at a huge evening banquet at a plantation some twelve miles from Bridgetown.

But the news was entirely false. Whilst the island partied into the night, the Parliamentary fleet under Sir George Ayscue, with George Marten and a number of the banished Roundhead planters on board, arrived off the beaches of Barbados. The very next day they sailed in to attack the defences of Bridgetown. Willoughby sent defiant messages, but Ayscue's patient policy of blockade and occasional raids wore down resistance. Reports of the final defeat of the Royalist cause at the battle of Worcester further eroded the Barbadians' will to fight. Eventually, after three months' effective siege, a large part of Willoughby's army commanded by Thomas Modyford defected and Willoughby was forced to come to terms. On 11 January 1652, talks began at the Mermaid Tavern at Oistins on Barbados's south-west coast, with William Byam among those negotiating for the Royalists.

An agreement was reached whereby the island was surrendered and a Roundhead governor installed. George Marten wrote to his brother, praising Ayscue, 'He has delivered us from the Lord Willoughby and those that with him meant to have raised their fortunes upon or by the ruin of this place.'

Perhaps reflecting the fact that the Royalist forces in Barbados still outnumbered those of Parliament, there were generous terms for Willoughby and his supporters, which included indemnity for all and, 'so long as he submits to the authority of the Commonwealth', specific permission for Willoughby to continue with his new colony in Suriname.

Yet just two months later, on 4 March 1652, contrary to the agreement, the leading Royalists were expelled from the island by the new Roundhead-dominated Assembly. 'Ordered to quit the island', Willoughby and Byam and other Cavaliers gathered what they could and embarked for their new domain, Willoughbyland.

Seven

'A BRAVE LAND'

'We stood on the borders of an enchanted land.'
SIR ROBERT SCHOMBURGK, *TRAVELS IN GUIANA*, 1840

The arriving party, led by Willoughby, was reported to have been as many as 300-strong, in three separate vessels. Though mainly from Barbados, some came directly, or very recently, from England. There were families with children, households with servants, freemen and women down on their luck or seeking a new start. Most of the Barbadians were Royalists, unwilling to live under the Parliamentary governorship of Puritan Daniel Searle whom Ayscue had installed in Barbados.

The newcomers, even though a majority were seasoned tropical-hands, were in for a shock. The natural world of Guiana had a richness, strangeness and fertility like nothing they had seen before. Europeans were used to perhaps, at most, 100 different species of tree; Guiana has 800. Sailing up the Orinoco, Walter Ralegh had noted 'flowers and trees of such variety as were sufficient to make ten volumes of

Herbals.' Almost all accounts of Willoughbyland comment on this extraordinary diversity. 'It is almost as easy to enumerate the stars of heaven as their several species of birds and beasts,' one visitor wrote, declaring the birds, of which there are a staggering 1,600 species, the most beautiful in the world.

The river, too, was home to hundreds, if not thousands, of different species, including over 300 different types of catfish and such novelties for the arriving Europeans as manatees, 'swordfish', caiman and giant otters. In the jungles roamed such exotics as anteaters, sloths and armadillos. No doubt, even today some creatures remain undocumented. In October 2013, scientists researching the ecosystems during a three-week expedition in Suriname's Upper Palumeu river watershed catalogued 1,378 species; they found sixty – including six frogs, one snake, and eleven fish – previously unknown. One Englishman who lived for three years in Willoughbyland in the 1660s wrote that someone could live there for far longer and 'yet be always finding some creature or other he had not met withal before.' There was even, he wrote, an insect that transformed itself into a plant. The overwhelming impact for the new arrivals was the feeling that here, even the most extraordinary things were possible.

At night, the noises of insects and frogs was 'so loud', one visitor wrote, 'that a man can hardly hear himself

*The wildlife of Willoughbyland, sometimes beautiful, sometimes deadly,
often both, gave the place an aura of strangeness and exoticism.*

speak, and the croakings of some of them are so horrid, that
do but imagine the latest groans of a dying person, and you
have it.'

It also felt hotter and more humid than Barbados, much
of which is cooled by sea breezes. With an annual average

91

rainfall in Suriname of 2,000mm, the damp got everywhere, rotting buildings, provisions and shoes. 'The heat,' one newcomer wrote, 'is something violent.' He was concerned that 'the constant breathing through the pores' meant that 'our spirits must make haste out of bodies exhaust by heat'.

Undaunted, however, the arriving settlers set to work. Those most senior marked out riverside plantations inland, planting tobacco (quick and easy to grow), provision grounds and terraces of lemon and mango trees. The poorer sort, without servants or substantial capital, ended up on the swampy, muddy ground near the sea where they were plagued by huge mosquitoes and ants, of which Suriname boasts the largest in the world.

A French priest, Antoine Biet, wrote an account of reaching Willoughbyland in late 1653, fifteen months after the arrival of the large body of settlers from Barbados. Biet had been part of the fourth or fifth French attempt to build a settlement on the Cayenne river. Five hundred settlers had embarked, but before they reached Cayenne at the end of September 1652, their leader had been assassinated in a mutiny, and there were bitter divisions between them. Once arrived, provisions ran low, an epidemic broke out and relations with the locals deteriorated into open war. Biet was one of the few who escaped by canoe; after a difficult voyage they found themselves out of food and water, but near the 'Anglois' settlement on the Suriname.

Biet was impressed with the new colony, noting that 'the English are very well established here.' The fort near the river mouth was well built, with outer walls of wood, but inside there was a small stone structure, impregnable to the weapons of the 'Indians'. Around the site of the fort two or three hundred acres of the land had been cleared. Here stood about fifty wooden buildings 'in native style, dotted about with no symmetry.'

According to the Frenchman, plantations growing tobacco or harvesting lumber now stretched up to thirty miles upriver. Biet was much taken by the riverbanks with their great trees, writing that there was 'nothing more beautiful in the world.'

He was also impressed with the cordiality of the welcome (once his party had handed over their arms) from Major Anthony Rous, the colony's leader. Willoughby himself had left on 2 June 1652, staying for only two months. He had returned to England to confirm his grant for Willoughbyland, define its borders and recover his English estates as had been promised as part of the generous terms for his surrender in Barbados. He would not return to his colony for a decade.

Initially, in his absence leadership seems to have been in the hands of Richard Holdip, a Barbados don. The records from this time are partial and fragmented, but it appears he was widely disliked for his 'cruelties', and, in Royalist-leaning Willoughbyland, for his Roundhead loyalties.

Then, in November 1652, Rous turned up in England demanding of the London authorities that he be made acting governor instead. The following month, Holdip's commission was revoked in favour of Rous, but it seems the first governor had already deserted his post. Rous returned to take up his position.

Back in Willoughbyland, Biet also wrote admiringly of William Byam, 'a worthy gentleman, in heart and word'. Byam, having been a sergeant major or at most a captain in Barbados, was now calling himself a colonel, and already appears to have become a key mover in the new colony. It was he who organised passes for the escaping Frenchmen to enter Willoughbyland and he also supplied the ship that sailed them on to Barbados. Biet notes that he had two plantations established upriver.

The experience of the French in Cayenne reminded everyone of the 'Indian danger'. We have, of course, no written records from the indigenous people of the region occupied by Willoughbyland. Anthropology and archaeology can aid speculation, but unhappily most of the information we have about them comes from the writing of English incomers. These accounts are sparse, far from impartial of course, and often contradictory. There is no doubt, though, that in respect of its indigenous people, Suriname was again very different from Barbados. There, the first settlers had encountered an empty place; there had been inhabitants in the past, but raids by Spanish slavers and other factors had seen the island deserted. However, soon after the colony was established, its founder Henry Powell had sailed to Guiana and landed at the Dutch settlement on the Essequibo river, which was led by a former shipmate of his, Amos van Groenewegen. Here Powell had persuaded some thirty indigenous people (labelled 'Arawaks' by the English) to return with him to Barbados to teach the raw settlers how to grow tropical staples such as cassava, 'Indian corn' (a type of maize) and yams. In return they were promised a piece of land, or a return trip home with £50 worth of axes, knives and other trade goods.

However, when in 1629 Powell lost a power struggle for control of Barbados, the Arawaks also lost their protector and found themselves enslaved, despite having saved the colony from starvation. When news of this outrage reached the Essequibo river, only the swift action of van Groenewegen in marrying a local girl prevented a furious uprising.

Richard Ligon, a Royalist refugee who sailed to Barbados with Thomas Modyford in 1647 and wrote a detailed account of the island, described the few 'Indians' he met there as 'much craftier, and subtler than the Negroes; and in their nature falser'. As well as Powell's contingent, there were a small number more 'fetched from other countries; some from the neighbouring islands, some from the Main, which we make slaves.' The women were employed as maids or in food growing and preparation, the men as footmen or fishermen, at which they were highly skilled.

In Willoughbyland, in contrast, the English were massively outnumbered. According to an account from the 1660s, there were some 5,000 'Carreeb' families living on the Suriname and the adjacent rivers, the Coppename, Saramacca and Commewine, with about 1,400 'Turroomacs' living in the interior.

Another account tells of 'several nations which trade and familiarly converse with the People of the colony', but 'those they live amongst are the Charibes, or Caniballs'. These lived off cassava bread and whatever of the plentiful fish or game they caught, going 'wholly naked, save a flap for modesty, which the women, after having had a child or two, throw off.' They slept on hammocks in low thatched cottages, with the eaves close to the ground, and by day had higher open-sided shelters.

'For ornament,' the report continues, 'they colour themselves all over into neat works, with a red paint called Anotta . . . They bore holes also through their noses, lips and ears, whereat they hang glass pendants, pieces of brass, or any such like baubles.' A different account noted, 'Indians are great lovers of fine gardens, drinking, dancing, and divers other pleasures.'

They lived 'like the Patriarchs of old', in large family groups 'where the eldest son always succeeds his father as the greatest.' But they also had 'Captains' who 'lead them out to wars.' The heads of families and higher 'Captains' would usually have three or four wives, and in general the men were waited on hand and foot by the women. Conflict between the various indigenous peoples was frequent, the weapons being bows and arrows and wooden clubs and 'for defence . . . shields made of light wood, handsomely painted and engraved.' Prisoners taken in war were either killed 'with the most barbarous cruelties' if they were men, or made slaves if women or children.

What emerges from the meagre and in parts unreliable sources of the relations between the English and their hosts is a complicated picture of alliances made and broken, supply of provisions proffered or withdrawn, of indigenous people employed as partners or held as slaves.

There were, of course, the 'two Indian kings' brought back to Barbados by Rous who had agreed to 'receive' the English 'to settle amongst them'. Nevertheless, there is a fleeting reference in one source to assaults on the first English settlers of Willoughbyland by hostile locals. These attacks, we learn, 'were always frustrated, and they profoundly smarted for their folly.' For this writer, who was in the colony early in the next decade, the 'Charibbes' were 'a people cowardly and treacherous', a verdict that chimes with Ligon's description from Barbados. But 'now the colony is grown potent,' he says, 'they dare not but be humble.'

Another writer who was there at the same time is given a different impression, however: 'we find it absolutely necessary to caress them as friends, and not to treat 'em as slaves; nor dare we do other, their numbers so far surpassing ours in that continent.'

In fact, the local 'captains' did sell their enslaved enemies to the English 'for trifles'. French priest Antoine Biet noted the presence of indigenous household slaves in the interior plantations. When a visitor in the 1660s took a trip upriver in a canoe, the craft was paddled by 'Indian slaves'. Still, the English had to be careful that they were not taking on slaves from supposedly friendly nearby tribes. There was even an expression – 'Beavers' – for those indigenous people it was safe to enslave. In general, it appears that the new English arrivals and the local 'Caribs' remained uneasy and loosely connected allies, while the upland groups remained altogether hostile. This was partly as they were now targets for enslavement by the coastal peoples, who then sold them to the English.

But as in Barbados, where an 'Indian' woman taught Richard Ligon how to make pastry out of cassava, the locals remained 'very useful', even essential to the English, particularly in the earliest years of the colony. Making cassava bread was a difficult and potentially dangerous process, as the poisonous juice of the root has to be carefully removed. One English visitor found the resulting bread, as well as the fellow staples of yams and plantains, almost entirely tasteless, but he was more taken with 'Perino', a drink made from fermented cassava, which tasted 'truly good, and nearly resembles our strongest March-Beer'. However, 'the relation of their manner of Brewing it', he goes on, 'will, I believe, rebate the edge of any one's desire'. The bread is baked until very black, at which point 'the oldest Women and snotty nose children chew [it] in their mouths, with as much Spittle as they can' before spitting it into a jar, and adding similarly chewed potatoes.

Although some food was imported from Virginia and New England, the local people also supplied the colonists with meat and fish. As in Barbados, they were expert fishermen; one visitor would call them 'Gods of the rivers . . . so rare an art they have in swimming, diving and almost living in the water.' They were also excellent shots with their bows and arrows, reportedly able to bring down oranges and other fruit too high in a tree to reach, shooting through the stalk, 'that they may not hurt the fruit'. Meat of all descriptions was hunted in the forests; Antoine Biet's party was presented by the locals with barbecued deer and hog.

There was, perhaps inevitably, another exchange between the English and their new hosts. The half-naked indigenous women were considered highly attractive by the Englishmen. Ralegh had found them 'excellently favoured', in particular the wife of a chief in the Orinoco valley, who was 'of good stature, with black eyes, fat of body, of an excellent countenance . . .

Indigenous inhabitants of Suriname, here depicted in a later French travelogue, fascinated incoming Europeans.

I have seldom seen a better favoured woman,' he wrote. Richard Ligon in Barbados had an Indian house slave who 'was of excellent shape and colour, for it was a pure bright bay; small breasts, with the nipples of a porphyrie colour, this woman would not be woo'd by any means to wear clothes.' George Warren, a writer who was in Willoughbyland in the 1660s, described the local indigenous women as 'generally lascivious, and some so truly handsome, as to features and proportion . . . their pretty bashfulness (especially while Virgins) in the presence of a stranger, adds grace to their perfections (too nakedly exposed to every wanton eye) that who ever lives amongst them had need be owner of no less than Joseph's continency, not at least to covet their embraces.'

There was a popular story doing the rounds at this time, which Ligon heard in Barbados and wrote down. Supposedly an English ship, in dire need of water and provisions, set a party down on the Guiana coast. They were ambushed and all but one killed. This survivor, 'straggling from the rest, was met by this Indian maid, who upon the first sight fell in love with him.' Called Yarico, she hid him from her countrymen in a cave, where she fed and cared for him, until they could safely return to the beach. From there they were both taken aboard the ship. 'But the youth, when he came ashore in Barbados, forgot the kindness of the poor maid, that had ventured her life for his safety, and sold her for a slave, who was as free born as he: And so poor Yarico for her love, lost her liberty.'

This story, with its melancholy romanticism, had somehow grabbed the imaginations of the English in the Caribbean, but of course, it wasn't all romance. There was no ban on fraternisation such as Ralegh had imposed on his men. Ligon's house slave soon 'chanced to be with child, by a Christian servant.' George Warren reported that one of the most common diseases suffered by the English settlers was 'the French-Pox . . . too frequently caught by coition with Indian-Women.' This behaviour was not the preserve of the common sort – William Byam himself is reported to have had an 'Indian mistress'.

*

As the number of English in the colony grew, up to 600 men as well as women and children by December 1654, dwarfing by a long way the failed colonies of Leigh and Harcourt, so the settlers could feel more secure. There was now, it seemed, 'perfect peace with the Indians'.

The colony was also in a 'flourishing condition'. For Thomas Modyford, who would prove in Jamaica to be perhaps England's canniest planter and colony builder, it was as if Ralegh's dream, ruined by the 'treachery of James I . . . and the base dullness of that age', was coming true. He now hoped, he wrote to London, that the men 'at the helme' would recognise the opportunities of 'one of the fertilist, most spacious and beautiful countries'. There were profits and national honour to be gained, trade to be increased, 'Indians' to be converted and employment secured for the 'great people' of England. 'It is a brave tract of land,' he went on, 'and if taken under the protection of the Commonwealth, would, in seven years, appear far more considerable than Brazil.'

Willoughby himself, in London wrangling over his grant, further argued – invoking Ralegh as well as appealing to Cromwell's anti-Spanish instincts – that the colony was so situated 'that from thence a strength may be easily conveyed into the bowels of the Spaniard at Peru.' Furthermore, the valuable pearl fisheries at Margarita could be attacked and 'Indians' all over the region encouraged in their resistance to Spain.

Willoughby was also recruiting new settlers for his colony. In 1655 he published in England an appeal, promising to provide vessels for those 'who are able & willing to transport themselves' at only £5 a head with accommodation 'according to their quality'. Children under ten were half price, infants free. On arrival every adult would be given fifty acres with thirty per child and twenty per servant in their employ.

Anyone 'serviceable & of good report' who could not afford the fare would be taken on as a servant of Willoughby himself and transported for free. Once in the colony, they would be bound for only four years, rather than the usual seven or more, with food, lodging and clothes provided. Once the term was completed, each would receive £10 and thirty acres. For those unable to pay the £5 but who were unwilling to indenture themselves, there were generous loans available, even though Willoughby had already spent a huge sum – as much as £20,000 – on establishing his colony. For those struggling to survive in post-war England, where times remained hard and the Commonwealth had degenerated into military rule, it seemed an excellent offer.

Willoughby also appealed for a new type of settler with the skills needed for a civil society moving beyond the pioneering stage – 'schoolmasters, physicians, surgeons, midwives, surveyors, architects, chemists' – to come with their 'books, instruments or tools'.

By 1656, the plantations reached sixty miles up the Suriname river, 'having overcome the hardship and great difficulty of a new settlement', as Willoughby declared. By now, he wrote, houses were built and provision grounds well established. So it was time for 'the planting of commodities' – cotton, tobacco, indigo, ginger, but, most importantly, sugar, 'being the hope which chiefly induced them to so far an adventure of so great difficulty and danger.'

Eight

'A PECULIAR FORM OF GOVERNMENT'

'You shall live freely there, without serjeants,
or courtiers, or lawyers, or intelligencers...
You may be an alderman there, and never be
a scavenger; you may be any other officer
and never be a slave.'

EASTWARD HOE ON AMERICA,
CHAPMAN, JONSON AND MARSTON, 1605

George Warren, the admirer of the 'truly handsome' indigenous women, published his *Impartial Description of Surinam* in 1667. He had spent three years in the colony working as a plantation manager, and was clearly much taken with the stunning beauty of the place, the wonderful fruit – in particular guavas and pineapples, 'the prince of fruits' – and the rich and varied wildlife. But he also gives his reader a warning: 'The delights of warm countries are mingled with sharp sauces.'

The founding of the colony had not been without heavy challenges. The first settlers, Warren reports, weakened by 'bad lodging and worse diet', succumbed in large numbers to 'feaver and ague'. Those servants who, due to the penury of their masters, were underfed, were vulnerable to 'dropsy', what we would now call oedema. The victim was rendered unable 'to expel those moist humours, which such tempers in that country do abundantly contract.' Another writer reports the prevalence of 'a certain sweating disease' that first caused numbness to the joints, followed by a burning fever.

Indeed, the forests and swamps of Suriname harboured blackwater and dengue fevers, cholera, typhoid and tuberculosis. Assassin bugs carried Chagas disease, and blackfly transmitted river blindness, caused by worms migrating to the eyeball. Sandfly bites – via the parasites they bore – could lead to a form of leprosy that ate away at the extremities. Warren warned that in the warm, wet climate, any 'sore', 'if not carefully look'd after', converted into a 'most loathsome and not easily cur'd mischief.'

Warren also devotes an entire chapter to 'Things there Venomous and Hurtful'. These include: 'snakes, crocodiles, scorpions, bats, ants, mosquitoes, toads, and frogs . . . The propagating heat has occasioned its swarming with so many several kinds of vermin.' Most to be feared were the snakes,

OPPOSITE: *A giant anaconda is hung on a branch to be skinned, from a book about Suriname published in England in the late eighteenth century.*

some of which, he writes, were nearly thirty feet long 'and of a greatness proportionable to their length'. These really big ones, though (almost certainly green anacondas), were slow and lacking venom, not nearly as dangerous as 'the lesser kinds', which were much more numerous and whose poison not only killed but caused 'the flesh in less than a day's space, to drop by piece-meal from the bones of them who are bitten'. This may refer to the haemotoxins carried in the venom of vipers and pit vipers, which is designed to begin the process of digestion of the victim by causing tissue degeneration and internal bleeding. During Warren's time at Willoughbyland, this was 'once or twice woefully experienced'. The deadliest of the pit viper family is the fer-de-lance, the most-feared snake in Suriname, partly because it has a habit of entering human dwellings in search of vermin. It multiplies prodigiously and its teeming young, though small, are extremely aggressive.

Scorpions, Warren explains, were not fatal, but caused severe pain for some hours. No one had died from the attentions of vampire bats, either, but some were driven from their homes, 'to save that little blood they had, which would have been sucked out.' However, two or three people had drowned while swimming in the river having encountered electric eels. These could deliver a shock of up to 600 volts, rendering the victim 'wholly useless and insensible'. There had also been several deaths from what Warren calls 'Tigers', and we'd call jaguars, living in the jungle. He tells the story of a settler who was lying in his hammock in his house when he was seized by a jaguar and carried into the forest. His shouts for help were heard by an Englishwoman living nearby, who fired a musket out of her window, but the noise failed to scare the jaguar into dropping his prey. The next day the man was found 'with his Head and Shoulders eaten off.'

Nevertheless, Warren remained undaunted, declaring that the country's 'blessings and advantages are of far greater weight' than any of these threats. This view was shared by most, and the colony was 'daily increasing', attracting many incomers, in large part from Barbados.

In 1653 the tiny island, less than 170 square miles, had a white population of some 26,000. Over the past decade, since the advent of sugar, small-scale farmers had been displaced by the large plantation owners; land had become prohibitively expensive for many; the places of white workers in the fields were being taken by more tractable and hardy enslaved Africans; and indentured servants who had finished their terms were no longer offered small plots of land – there was none to spare.

There were other 'push' factors driving emigration from Barbados to Willoughbyland. After control was taken of the island by Ayscue, new rules had been imposed by London designed to make the colonies benefit the mother country: no colonial produce could be shipped to England except in vessels owned and for the most part manned by Englishmen;

European goods could not be imported by the colonies except in English ships or those of the country where the goods were produced.

This Navigation Act, effectively establishing an English monopoly on trade with England and its colonies, was widely ignored, but still strongly rankled. The Barbados planters were quick to point out their heavy debt to the Dutch who had been so instrumental in establishing the lucrative sugar business on the island, supplying equipment and know-how, and labour in the form of slaves. Furthermore, the Dutch sold goods from Europe far cheaper than English merchants, who now used their monopoly to hike up their prices further.

It was a controlling measure contrary to everything the Barbadians wanted. While waiting for the Parliamentary fleet to arrive, Willoughby himself had made an extraordinary pronouncement of colonial autonomy on behalf of Barbados, which now seems strikingly similar to the American Declaration of Independence of 140 years later. Why should Barbados obey 'a Parliament in which we have no Representatives, or persons chosen by us?' he asked. He continued, 'In truth this would be a slavery far exceeding all that the English nation hath yet suffered.' In 1652, the island, in the person of Thomas Modyford, repeated the suggestion – 'though it might seem immodest' – that it send two MPs to London, while reports were heard in London that there were people in Barbados who sought 'to make this place a free state, and not run any fortune with England, either in peace or war'. In the meantime, members of the Assembly sought to diminish the power of the London-appointed governor, and wrest control from the executive of the militia and other public bodies.

Willoughbyland was entirely different. There, free trade lived on, and the effective independence the Barbadians desired was a reality. The colony was ignored by Cromwell, who had more pressing concerns, at home and abroad, including war with Spain and, from 1655, the after-effects of the ramshackle conquest of Jamaica. These prevented him from taking measures to bring Suriname effectively within the bounds of his empire. In fact, because of the settlers' Royalist leanings, it would have been difficult to send out from England a governor who would at the same time remain loyal to the Protector and be able to control the colonists without armed support, which with demands elsewhere, could not be provided from England.

Willoughby's efforts at establishing his authority were also stalled. In March 1654 the Council in London had recommended that letters patent for proprietorship of Suriname be issued to him and his heirs, as had been promised by the Mermaid Tavern Agreement. This would have given Willoughby absolute power in the colony – to appoint a governor, write and enforce laws and collect revenue – but the matter had hung fire. So the colony was in limbo, free to go its own way, especially after 1654 when the London-appointed acting governor Anthony Rous left the colony seemingly to return to the life of a soldier. (He turns up in Jamaica the following year during the English invasion, then last appears in the record living in Barbados in 1661.)

For three years there was no discernible leadership, beyond that of individual planters over their own households. In late 1655, the governor of Barbados reported that the 'colony of Surranam' was without 'any person authorized in the government amongst them.'

However, by 1657, the colonists had organised themselves: there was a small militia made up of the poorer whites officered in the main by their plantation-owning superiors; there was also a form of representative government, with an assembly of twenty-one men chosen by and from the colony's wealthier male landowners, and a six-man council appointed by the governor. The governor and council administered justice and proposed measures – such as raising money for defence or building a prison – that would then be voted on by the assembly, who would meet every few months, usually in one of the larger plantation houses. But whereas in places like Barbados the governor would be appointed either by the proprietor or by the government in London, here he was subject to annual elections. In 1657, this was won by William Byam, by then in his mid-thirties. This 'peculiar kind of Government . . . elective in the people' was highly attractive to freedom-loving Barbadians.

Of the hundreds of Barbadians and other West Indians who now flocked to Willoughbyland, most were Cavalier by sympathy. But there were also a significant number of Roundheads. The most politically noted was George Marten, whom Willoughby in 1650 had sent from Barbados to try to broker a peace with Parliament in England. Marten had returned with the Parliamentary fleet and become a pillar of the Barbados community, a trustee of the vestry of St John's parish (although he would later be accused of atheism, blasphemy and debauchery) and from 1655 speaker of the assembly, from which position he had been in the forefront of efforts to reduce the power of the London-appointed governor.

With borrowed money, he had started growing sugar and by 1656 had 250 acres in cane. But he failed to repay the debts and the land was reclaimed by his creditors. In 1658 he abandoned Barbados for Willoughbyland, where he took on a plantation about three days' journey by river from Paramaribo. For now, the new Roundhead arrivals seem to have got on fine with the Cavaliers. It was a return to the days of the jokey turkey-dinner forfeit in Barbados.

The other large group of new arrivals were Jews. According to some reports, Willoughby had brought a number of

Jewish families with him when he arrived in March 1652, and certainly there was a large influx two years later from Brazil. In 1654 Recife was reconquered by the Portuguese after twenty-four years of Dutch occupation. The Dutch had given the many people of Jewish descent unprecedented freedom of worship and commerce, but the return of the Portuguese ended this, so many hundreds upped sticks for the north-west, finding in Willoughbyland a not-so-dissimilar body of freedom-loving, tolerant and independent refugees. Attractions offered by the English to the Jews were freedom of conscience, the right to erect a synagogue (the first of which was built in 1654), eligibility for election as burgesses, passage to Holland in Dutch vessels, and from seven to twelve years' exemption from taxation. No doubt it was remembered how useful the Jewish transatlantic trading and banking links had been for establishing the sugar industry in Barbados. But it was also part of a wider tolerant, egalitarian and optimistic spirit in the colony through the 1650s.

Nowhere else before the nineteenth century had Jews enjoyed so many political privileges with so little intrusion into their lives. The result was the first permanent Jewish settlement in the Americas; today the ruins of the oldest stone-built synagogue in the western hemisphere are still to be found up the Suriname river.

Jewish settlement was concentrated in the 'Jewish Savannah' (now Joden Savanne), the comparatively unjungled and sandy belt of land on the river about fifty miles inland as the crow flies. Byam's estates were just a little downriver from here. In general the centre of gravity of the colony had moved upriver. As a result, Torarica became the main town. Situated a little south of Jewish Savannah, it stood on the west side of the Suriname, where the river widens considerably as it takes a sharp turn to the east, providing space for numerous ships – of up to 300 tons – to anchor. Here English, French and Dutch vessels arrived with machinery, clothes and shoes, luxury goods, food and wine, and took away sugar, molasses and rum as well as dyes, precious woods, tobacco and cotton. Ships from New England and Virginia brought barrels of salted fish and meat as well as oxen, cattle and horses.

Willoughby himself had a large estate called Parham Hill, upriver of Torarica. Here he seems to have ordered that his employees dig into the mountain to look for gold. There is no surviving evidence that he was in touch with Governor William Byam or influencing his government and Willoughby still failed to make an appearance in his colony. Instead, he remained in London, continuing unsuccessfully to lobby to be given official proprietorship. Seemingly rebuffed, he threw himself into plotting the return of the King. In 1654, Charles II wrote to Willoughby telling him 'to be ready upon any great occasion', and the following year Willoughby was active in preparing for a Royalist uprising. In June 1655 he was imprisoned by Cromwell, then again in September 1656. On both occasions he was only freed thanks to the intervention of the influential Sir Martin Noell and Thomas Povey. Noell, as well as being related to Willoughby, was a financier who had backed a number of Cromwell's schemes with a view to then being given the right to farm the customs revenue. He was almost certainly a key backer of Willoughby's investment in Suriname. His half-brother Thomas Noell, a plantation owner and sergeant major in the militia, was living in Willoughbyland, and a 1667 plantation map also has land marked as owned by Sir Martin.

Thanks to Noell's efforts, and perhaps also with a view to getting the troublesome man out of the country, Willoughby was released in November 1657 on condition that he give security of £10,000 and remove himself to Suriname, to 'enjoy the settlements already made by him there, according to the articles granted on the surrender of Barbados.' This effectively gave him what he wanted at last, yet he still remained in England and continued to plot. He was active again in the summer of 1659 as a member of the Sealed Knot, a secret Royalist organisation. He was one of the leaders of what became the failed Booth's Uprising. According to the plan, Willoughby was to secure East Anglia for the plotters. However, agents of the formidable government spymaster Thomas Scot had infiltrated the conspiracy, and the uprising was stillborn.

Cromwell had died in September 1658, and his son and nominated successor Richard, showing neither the ability nor the inclination to rule, and lacking the support of the army, had stood down in May 1659. There followed a period of struggle between the army and various Parliaments and within the army itself, which culminated in General Monck, the military governor of Scotland, marching south with his personal force of 10,000 men to 'see my country freed from that intolerable slavery of a sword government'. Wanting neither anarchy nor military rule, a new Parliament organised by Monck voted on 1 May 1660 for a return of the monarchy.

The navy's finest ship, the *Naseby*, hastily renamed the *Royal Charles*, was sent to collect Charles II from the continent. He landed at Dover on 25 May. With his return, Willoughby's star was set to rise.

By this time, Willoughbyland, while by some distance the most successful Guiana colony yet with over a thousand settlers, was still the most independent corner of the empire, unaccustomed to taking orders from anyone. Not everyone there would welcome the return of its founder's power.

The 'Musica' or 'El Dorado Raft', discovered in 1969, suggests that the El Dorado legend originated in a ceremony held by the Musica people on a lake in the Columbian Andes.

An engraving from 1599 showing Sir Walter Ralegh's capture of Antonio de Berrío in Trinidad. Only one other Spaniard was spared execution. In the background, the new town of San José de Oruña is in flames.

OPPOSITE: *Sir Walter Ralegh and his son Wat, then aged eight, showing determined faces to an unknown artist in 1602. The following year Ralegh was imprisoned in the Tower of London.*

RIGHT: *Francis Lord Willoughby, 5th Baron of Parham. Having created Willoughbyland, he was largely absent from its short life. His eventual, calamitous return brought dissension and plague.*

The liuelie Effigies of that noble Lord Willoughbie de Parham.

A map of 1633 showing El Dorado. The imagined lake – Parime Lacus – and city on its north-west tip continued to appear on maps of the region into the nineteenth century.

Stedman *T. II. Tav. IV.*

OPPOSITE: *Aphra Behn painted by Sir Peter Lely in the 1670s at the height of her fame.*

RIGHT: *A 'Carib' family, as depicted by a Scotsman in Suriname in the eighteenth century. An earlier visitor warned that the Carib men could 'loose ten or a dozen arrows in the time it takes to load a gun.'*

FAMIGLIA INDIANA CARAIBA.

The extraordinary natural world of Suriname, painted by German-born naturalist Maria Merian and published in 1705. One of Ralegh's ill-fated companions in 1617 declared the Guianas 'an earthly paradise ... full of fruitful promise.'

A map of Willougbyland drawn in 1667, showing the Suriname river and its tributaries, as well as the position of the plantations all along the river banks.

ABOVE: *30 December 1666: the Dutch fleet under Admiral Crijnssen sets sail to attack Willoughbyland.*

RIGHT: *Sir John Harman, in a series of victories, reversed the balance of naval power in the Caribbean in 1667–8. But his recapture of Willoughbyland came too late.*

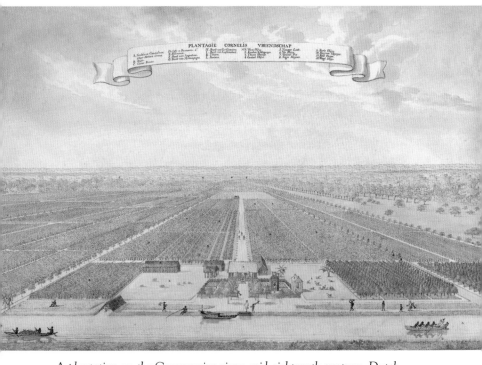

A plantation on the Commewine river, mid-eighteenth century. Dutch drainage expertise converted the neglected coastal 'drowned lands' of the English colony into an agricultural goldmine.

The jungled banks of the Suriname river today.

Nine

THE RESTORATION: 'A TUMBLING AND ROLLING WORLD'

'O England, England, England, England,
what hast thou done?'

QUAKER DANIEL BAKER, FROM WORCESTER GAOL, 1660

Watching the cheering crowds greeting the King as he entered London on 29 May 1660, Royalist John Evelyn noted the 'inexpressible joy; the ways strewed with flowers, the bells ringing, the streets hung with tapestry, fountains running with wine.' There had never been, he wrote, 'so joyful a day and so bright ever seen in this nation.' Another Londoner wrote to a friend in Paris more wryly, 'Were you here, you would say, good God! Do the same people inhabit England that were in it ten or twenty years ago?'

Of course, these were in large part the same people who had cheered the execution of Charles I, now eager to demonstrate their new-found Royalism. In fact, the country would remain fractious and divided for many years. People wanted stability and an end to the deep divides and endless political and ecclesiastical disputes. Still, there were many deeply unwilling to give up their hard-won new religious and political freedoms as the old power structure of King, court, lords and bishops returned.

The revolutionary period had seen an extraordinary fertility in political ideas. In February 1652, 'Digger' leader Gerrard Winstanley had dedicated to Cromwell a pamphlet that suggested the establishment of a collectivist society in which everyone worked for the good of all under the superintendence of overseers elected by the community. Other pamphleteers had demanded the disestablishment of the Church, a single-chamber republic, the abolition of rotten boroughs, freedom of the press, freedom of trade, reform of the law, women's suffrage and the formation of a national bank. Two decades of unprecedented social, political and religious upheaval could not be forgotten that quickly.

Thus, contrary to Charles II's reputation as the 'merry monarch', his return saw the beginning of a period of ruthless repression. Acts passed by the Royalist Cavalier Parliament restored the rule of the oligarchy over the merchants, tradesmen and even labourers who had been seeking and achieving agency in government; the series of laws known as the Clarendon Code launched the most sustained persecution of Nonconformists in English history; popular education, seen as guilty of giving people ideas above their station, was returned to the dead hand of the Established Church; the University of Oxford was busy burning treatises by the likes of Hobbes and Milton.

In an attempt to put the genie back in the bottle, full-scale censorship was imposed, and newspapers were banned with the exception of government sheets. No book, pamphlet or periodical could be published without an official stamp that showed that nothing inside was 'contrary to the Christian faith . . . or against the state or government of this realm or contrary to good life or manners.' The number of master printers in England was allowed to dwindle to twenty, after which none was to be admitted to the Stationers' Company except with the approval of the Archbishop of Canterbury and the Bishop of London. Soon there were officially no printing presses outside London, Oxford and Cambridge.

Nevertheless, these measures failed to choke off the propagation of radical ideas from press or pulpit. According to the officer charged with hunting them down, underground presses churned out some 300 treasonous books or pamphlets in the four years after 1660. Several were prosecuted, including one, John Twyn, for printing a pamphlet justifying the execution of Charles I. Pressed to reveal the name of the pamphlet's anonymous author (and thereby save his own life), Twyn refused, later telling the prison chaplain that 'it was not his principle to betray the Author.' As a result he suffered the penalty for treason of being hanged, drawn and quartered, which included castration and disembowelment while still alive. A fellow printer accused at the trial was Thomas Brewster, who had reproduced the defiant scaffold speeches of those who had signed Charles I's death warrant. He was imprisoned and pilloried, as a result of which he died. More than 3,000 mourners attended his funeral in April 1664.

This public display of support was testament to the growing unpopularity of the Restoration regime. The execution of the regicides had created noble martyrs; there were onerous new taxes and the sale of Dunkirk to the French in 1662 was seen as betrayal. The court was widely viewed as spendthrift, licentious and immoral. While sailors of the Royal Navy went unpaid, Charles II spent thousands of pounds on jewels for his Queen and mistresses.

Thus radical activity, including uprisings and numerous plots, continued through the 1660s. None succeeded, hampered in part by the internal divisions of the opposition to the King, but Charles's officials had to maintain constant vigilance. In August 1663 a plot based in Yorkshire was discovered. Some conspirators were arrested, others fled to Holland; twenty or so of those captured, mostly old Republicans, were hanged. It turned out that government agents had infiltrated the conspiracy. In the bitterly divided realm, secrecy became endemic. Spies and informers were everywhere.

Francis Willoughby was handsomely rewarded for his years of plotting for the King. In recognition of the seven years still to run on his lease from Carlisle, on 9 July 1660 he was reinstated to the plum position of Royal Governor of the 'Caribbees': Barbados, St Kitts, Nevis, Montserrat and Antigua.

Willoughby did not, as instructed, leave for Barbados to take up his new position, but yet again stayed in London negotiating royal recognition of his proprietorship of Willoughbyland. On the same day that he was appointed governor of the Caribbees, a warrant had been made out to grant him 'Guiana, in America, to be held of the manor of East Greenwich'. By Guiana, it was meant all the land between the Orinoco and Amazon rivers. But before the warrant could pass the seals, objections were made, probably by Edward Hyde, Earl of Clarendon, Charles's effective first minister. While no one disputed Willoughby's claim as 'first settler', nor denied the huge amount of money he had personally invested in the venture, was not such an unprecedentedly vast grant – 1,200 miles in length and 600 in breadth – too much for one man? Would it not be a 'great grievance to the inhabitants to be given away from the Crown'?

The scope of the grant was reduced, but still objections delayed its approval. Then Willoughby did a deal with Clarendon. The proprietorship would be shared with his twenty-one-year-old second son Lawrence Hyde, a man seemingly without merit for the role and clearly a sleeping partner. Objections were withdrawn and at last, on 6 May 1663, letters patent from the King were issued. The 'Willoughbyland' granted to 'Francis Lord Willoughby and Lawrence Hyde, their heirs and assigns' as 'true and absolute Lords, Proprietors and Governors' would be a territory bordered by the Coppename and Maroni rivers, approximately the eastern half of modern-day Suriname. The extent of the interior was left vague – to the heads of the rivers and the 'South Sea'. The King was to have 30,000 acres reserved as royal demesne, 2,000 pounds' weight of tobacco yearly, the fifth of the proceeds of any 'gold or silver gotten there' (still a great hope), and two white horses, to be presented whenever he or any of his successors visited the country. It was also ordered that the proprietors build towns and cities, equipped with fairs, markets, colleges and 'schools of good Literature'.

In the climate of the time, this was highly exceptional. The Restoration government's attitude was to rein in the colonies, tie them closer to the home country and have them operate to England's benefit. To this end, in the 'Caribbees', proprietorial government was ended in favour of direct rule under a royal governor, in this case Willoughby. In return for recognising the sometimes dubious nature of the planters' land tenures on the West Indian islands, Charles demanded 4.5 per cent export duty. In theory the money was for colonial government, but in reality Charles spent the money in England or it went to Willoughby himself or creditors of the old proprietor.

In addition, the Interregnum Navigation Act was reissued with stricter terms, tying the colonials to exclusive trade with England in English vessels. But for Willoughbyland, an exception from these rules was made and export duty was not demanded as elsewhere: 'free trade, without custom'. No doubt secured by Clarendon in the financial interest of his son, the exemptions gave Willoughbyland a huge advantage over its English-ruled competitors. So while the strict imposition of the Navigation Act added costs on exports and saw prosperity slump in Barbados and the other islands, Suriname boomed.

Although it is still poorly documented, we know a little bit more about the Suriname colony as it moves into the 1660s from the accounts of a handful of European settlers and visitors. Almost all comment on the enduring appeal of the El Dorado story, one declaring, 'It is most certain that there is both gold, silver and emerald in many of the Countries on or adjacent to the Amazones.' George Warren reports stories of a country of 'Ancient learned heathens' in the interior, but with a degree of cynicism: 'The Indians will tell you of mighty Princes upwards, and Golden Cities, how true I know not.' This interior remained inaccessible; where the rapids began – on the Suriname a few miles south of Parham Hill – so European penetration ended. On one occasion, a well-armed group of white settlers set off in pursuit of upland indigenous people who had killed a European woman and robbed her house. 'With most grievous labour' they hauled their boats by land up as many as eight waterfalls, but 'were at last, compell'd to return without desired Success, not have so much as seen an Indian . . . some of them were dash'd to pieces in the Descent.'

The very inaccessibility of the hinterland continued to fuel European imagination as to what unknown wonders might be found there and to tempt the brave or foolish to venture inland. Such were the losses from these expeditions that a visitor in the mid-1660s reported that Willoughby even wrote to order guards to be set on the rivers to prevent them, 'because all the Country was mad to be going on this Golden Adventure.'

Pioneers from elsewhere kept up the search too: expeditions under the Ghent-born explorer Mathies Matteson had ventured far inland from the Orinoco in 1655 and, most recently, in 1661 up the Essequibo river, in search of the mythical city. Even the otherwise down-to-earth Dutch merchant, van Groenewegen, who had made such a success of the trading station on the Essequibo, was gripped by the idea, making numerous forays inland, the last being in 1661.

In Suriname, though, this was no longer the priority for most of its inhabitants. Some years later a Jamaican plantocrat was asked why he did not make any effort to find the island's reputed gold mines. He replied, surveying his waving fields of sugar cane, 'While we have so profitable a mine above ground we will not trouble for hunting for one underground.' So it now was in Willoughbyland. The accounts from the 1660s depict a thriving, mixed agricultural economy, benefiting from fresh soil and seemingly boundless space.

John Trefry was a young Cornishman who was managing the upriver estate called Parham Hill for its owner, the absent Willoughby. In 1662 he reported, 'Our colony is daily improving. Seven ships have already gone hence laden with specklewood and other commodities.' Specklewood (*Piratinera guianensis*) is also known as snakewood. The trunk is mostly soft white sapwood, but at its centre is a billet of lustrous, wine-red heartwood, shot through with striking dark markings. Although very hard and difficult to work, it was in great demand for veneers, fetching 'thirty or forty pounds a ton'. Other hardwoods, many known as ironwood or *Lignum vitae*, were also being exported to be made into furniture as well as mill rollers and other industrial machinery.

Different trees and shrubs – logwood, fustic, annatto – were harvested for the dye-hungry European linen industry, shipped, in the main, to the United Provinces for processing. The Dutch had also mastered the art of blending cheap home-grown tobacco with choicer tobaccos from Brazil, the Caribbean or Virginia. The tobacco from Suriname was considered of the highest quality, better even than that of Virginia. Other commodities of the country listed in a report of the 1660s include honey, rice, wax, 'Rich gums, balsoms, many Phisickall Drugs', and cotton. According to Warren, the last did not grow as well inland as on the islands because of the excessive rains, and being too far distant from sea, whose 'brackish dew' kept off the caterpillars.

News of the colony's success was spreading. In May 1662, *Mercurious Publicus* informed its English readership, 'Surynam . . . first settled in time of rebellion by banished Royalists is yet coming to the highest probability of being the richest and healthfullest of all our foreign settlements.' In August the following year a government official, Renatus Enys, arrived to take stock of the colony. He reported a white population of 4,000, which was growing weekly with new incomers and with 'succeeding generation, for the women are very prolifical and have lusty children.' Trade was booming with ships from many nations arriving every week. As well as the exports above, he noticed that the breeding of cattle was now under way. 'The chiefest commodity' though, he determined, was sugar, 'and better cannot be made'.

Trefry had boasted that 'our sugar is far better, and of greater price than that of Barbados,' a claim repeated by Enys and Warren. Trefry also reported that the colony's first windmill for driving the cane-crushing equipment had recently come into operation on the estate of Sergeant Major Noell. Trefry hoped to have one completed at Parham Hill very soon.

Sugar required substantial capital investment. The processing infrastructure – mill, boiling house, curing house, distillery – had to be built and equipped on site as the juice of the canes, once cut, quickly fermented. The pattern across the Caribbean was for planters to proceed to sugar through stages. In Suriname, land was cleared by felling during the months from April to August, and at the end of September, usually a rare dry period, it was burnt, with the ashes enriching the soil. Usually the land would then be planted in pea crops or 'Indian corn' while the stumps rotted, then root crops such as yams, with perhaps ginger or indigo (although the latter was, like sugar, difficult to process). Then, in the third year, the land was ready for sugar cane, with the hope that the minor crops had produced sufficient profit to build the necessary sugar factory. Planting of provisions would then be moved to higher ground.

By 1665, there were plantations along both sides of the Suriname river as far as Armadillo Hill, and also along

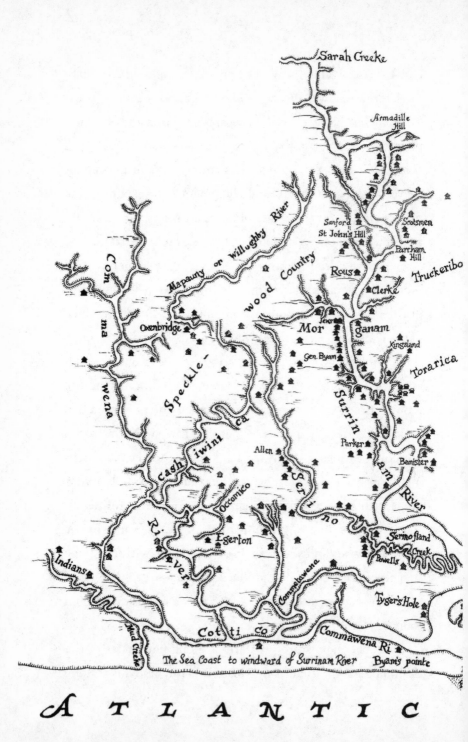

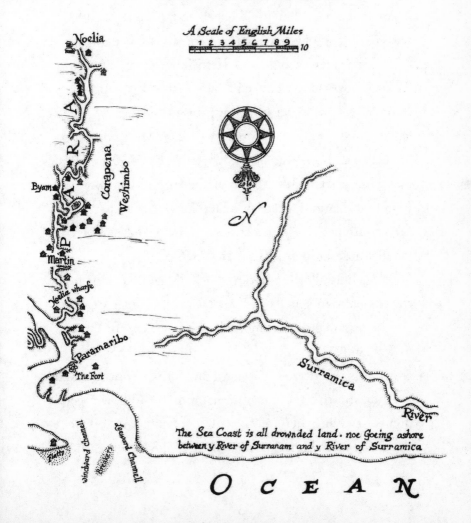

A Discription of the Colony of Surranam in Guiana
-: Drawne in the yeare 1667 :-
(Redrawn by Emmy Lopes, 2015)

The Plantations as they are Settled in the
Severall parts of the Country.
The land is low and very full of woods;
it is very Bad travelling from one
Plantation to an other without Boats.

A Scale of English Miles
1 2 3 4 5 6 7 8 9 10

N

Noelia

PRARA

Corapena

Weshimbo

Byam

Martin

Noelia wharfe

Paramaribo

The Fort

Surramica River

Flatts

windward channell

Breakers

Leeward Channell

The Sea Coast is all drownded land . noe Goeing ashore
between y River of Surranam and y River of Surramica

O C E A N

its tributaries, the Serino and Corapena. In all there were nearly two hundred plantations of which forty or fifty now had sugar works 'yielding no small profit to the Owners'. Warren reckoned that in a few years, the sugar businesses generated more profit than 'is usually produc'd from a greater foundation, and more continued industry in England.'

Torarica had also grown populous, with a hundred houses, a government building, a chapel and a large, well-built harbour. Many of the incomers were still from Barbados – up to sixty a day according to Trefry. Enys reported that the 'Dons of Barbados' did their best to stop this emigration, using 'their utmost means to disparage the country'. Their 'chief interest' was to hold on to Barbados's white population 'to balance the power of the negroes'. By 1660 enslaved Africans, at some 30,000, outnumbered the whites on the island, an alarming state of affairs for the colonisers. But, Enys continues, 'their hypocrisies are discovered, and several families are transporting thither.'

As well as allowing free trade, Willoughby's grant from the King also included freedom of worship – 'liberty to such as inhabit said province and cannot conform to the Church of England'. This allowance, together with the colony's growing prosperity, saw Jewish immigration continue and grow during the 1660s. Petitions from 1661 show a good number arriving then (along with a group of Quakers), but the greatest Jewish influx came in 1664. Five years earlier a large party of Jews fled Brazil during the Dutch-Portuguese War and settled in Cayenne, abandoned by the French in 1652, and now under loose Dutch control. When the French returned in 1664 and expelled the Dutch, the Jewish community, led by David Nassy, relocated en masse to Suriname, the majority joining the settlement at Jewish Savannah. The following year a grant of privileges issued by the Willoughbyland governor and assembly restated the policy of allowing religious freedom for the Jewish community, as well as permission to set up their own courts for minor suits, and ten acres of land at Torarica for the erection of a synagogue and schools. The Jews, it was announced, 'have, with their persons and property, proved themselves useful and beneficial to this colony.'

The promise of religious freedom was also a powerful draw for immigrants from England. There, the Clarendon Code had resulted in persecution of Nonconformists as well as hundreds of preachers being thrown out of their livings. One such was John Oxenbridge, who had arrived in Suriname by 1662 and, according to a plantation map of 1667, took on land near the southern extremity of the colony. He would write a missionary tract, *A Seasonable Proposition of Propagating the Gospel by Christian Colonies in the Continent of Guiana.*

Describing himself as a 'silly worm, too inconsiderable for so great a work', his emphasis was on recruiting fellow Nonconformists from England to help spread the Word. Guiana, he wrote, was 'apt for the endeavour', with picturesque 'Indians', industrious, ingenious and humane (and much less fierce than those in Florida), and a climate that offered an escape from the 'rough assaults of a hoary, horrid winter' to 'the cherishing wings of the Sun, that their spirits may have a more lightsome house to work in for their Lord.'

Not only would those joining his work store up riches for the next world, 'but even in this; for ye know not what ye may need, & how soon, in a tumbling and rolling world; wherefore adventure something and let not doubtfull events hinder you,' he wrote. Willoughbyland, with its rich soil, could give the bold a fortune to cushion them, for who knew what the ongoing effects of the Restoration of the King would be at home for people of independent spirit?

Just as the remoteness and neutrality of the West Indies had attracted Cavaliers during the Civil Wars and Interregnum, so it now appealed to Parliamentarians and radicals. They combined with the second wave, non-Cavalier immigrants from Barbados, to form a sizeable anti-Royalist group in the colony.

Oxenbridge offers many more enticements: plentiful timber made building materials cheap; the food was 'here in greater plenty and variety than in England or any of its Plantations elsewhere settled'; the country abounded with 'Nutmeg-trees, cinnamon, cloves, several sorts of pepper'; for 'further refreshing' there were figs, oranges, lemons, limes, pomegranates, pineapples, guavas, dates, almonds, cacao, 'and several sorts of plums'.

Nonetheless, his enthusiastic manifesto does contain one note of regret. For such an Edenic new world, he laments, the 'Seed-corn should not be the refuse, but choicest of corn'. In fact, some of the conduct of his fellow settlers was a 'Scandall of Christian Religion'.

Another Nonconformist pamphleteer, Henry Adis, was even harsher in his description of Suriname society, written at the end of 1663. The colony was peopled by a 'rude rabble', he declared, given to 'lascivious Abominations', 'bitter oaths and horrid execrations'. Many English in the colony, though they called themselves Christian, were in fact, he wrote, 'by their debauched Atheistic Actions . . . more brutish by far, than the very Heathens themselves.' Adis urged a 'thorough Reformation'.

The proprietor, Willoughby himself, responded to these complaints, admitting that new colonies were usually made up of rough types, but that he hoped in time that Suriname would become more 'civilly bred . . . All new colonies you know of what sort of people generally they are made up of.'

George Warren also hints that the Suriname planters, far from home and threatened with an early death from disease or 'Carib' attack, lived fast. He reckoned that Willoughbylanders 'decay more quickly than in these Northern Countries.' It did not help that men, women and children were 'much addicted to the Pipe', and tobacco was burnt everywhere to deter the incessant, numberless mosquitoes.

Government officer Renatus Enys's 1663 report back to London on the colony was almost all favourable. He had found the inhabitants generous and obliging, the country 'exceeding fruitful' and 'the natives not numerous, and at peace with the white incomers.' 'Were the English nation really informed of the goodness of this country,' he declared, 'there would quickly be thousands of settlers.' In fact, he concluded, Willoughbyland was the most 'hopeful' colony in the empire, in addition to its perfect position 'for any design against the Spaniard'.

There was a note of caution, however. Although Enys reported the colony's 'good order, being nobly upheld by the power and prudence of those at the helm', there was great hope that Lord Willoughby would 'suddenly' arrive, and the colony would be '"bottomed" on Royal authority, the want of which', Enys writes, 'has given encouragement to incendiaries . . . The chief of these have given a liberty to their tongues, pens, and press to sully this colony with variety of lies . . .'

Trefry also notes that 'we have long been in expectation of my Lord Willoughby'. He, too, hints that there was serious trouble on the way.

Ten

REPRESSION AND REVOLT

'Who overcomes
By force, hath overcome but half his foe.'
JOHN MILTON, *PARADISE LOST*

William Byam had been re-elected as governor in both 1658 and 1659, and had used his time in charge to build up a substantial 'faction' of supporters in the assembly. He interpreted the Restoration and the return of autocracy in England as giving him free rein in Suriname. The first we hear of it is when in October 1660 Byam had a carpenter, Daniel Jones, put in irons for 'abusing the authority of the colony' and for his 'insufferable insolence'. Jones's friend Michael Mashart pleaded for him to be released on bail, but Byam refused. Jones then escaped and with Mashart took off armed into the woods.

The 'incendiaries' most probably referred to by Enys, however, were the Sanford brothers. William Sanford was a member of the council and his brother Robert was an assembly member and lieutenant colonel in the militia.

From a complaint that Robert Sanford wrote to London about William Byam, we know that Robert had come out to the West Indies as a young boy (he apologises to his reader for his awkward idiom, having been away from England for more than twenty years). William and Robert appear to have come to Willoughbyland from Barbados, where they were linked to the Roundhead faction led by the first sugar baron, James Drax. (Robert Sanford later claimed that Drax encouraged him in his battle with Byam.) There was a plantation in the family name near Willoughby's Parham Hill, which might have originated from a Sanford uncle 'well interested in Surinam'. The Sanfords were part of a group of planters who were concerned about the legal status of their land tenure under the new proprietorship, and saw the uniqueness of Willoughbyland – described by Robert Sanford as its 'peculiar kind of Government . . . elective in the people' – under threat from the changed circumstances of the Restoration.

Clearly, some of the Suriname planters, particularly those of an anti-Royalist disposition, saw Willoughby's proposed power over the colony as excessive, even monstrous. Part of his royal grant gave him or his appointee responsibility to administer justice, including the death penalty. It seemed that Willoughby himself, and his establishment in Suriname, was above the law. Wasn't this the mistake that Charles I had made and been punished for?

To preserve order at home, plans had been made by Parliament three weeks before Charles II landed at Dover, that officials such as sheriffs, mayors and constables should continue with their duties in the King's name. Rumours of this reached Byam in Suriname at the same time as he learnt of the return of the King. He then claimed to have received a similar order to keep in his post, even though his year's office had only a month to run. Byam 'pretendeth to have his Majesty's proclamation, but never showeth it', Sanford complained. Instead, Sanford continued, the order was but 'a meer Chimera of Byam's own Brain, invented to serve his Ambition for a Perpetual Dominion'.

However, for Byam, the return of the King had changed everything. Defending himself, he later wrote, 'Here democracy fell, by the loyal concessions to monarchy.' In May 1661 Byam and his tame assembly voted that they should continue in office until further instructions came from home. In the circumstances, they decided, the scheduled fresh elections would 'be but a needlesse and unnecessary Charge and Trouble to the inhabitants.' But even if the assembly was compliant, opposition grew, with 'the generality, robbed of their privileges', beginning to 'mutter, and others better spirited openly deny his power.' The 'subject', Sanford complained, 'that hazards life, and fortunes to enlarge his Majesty's dominions, the revenue of his crown, and the traffic of the nation, deserves not to be disenfranchised.' Byam only cancelled the election because he knew he was going to lose, Sanford alleged. Both sides accused the other of 'sloth and drunkenness'.

The undercurrent of muttering dissatisfaction came to a head in October at a meeting of the residents of Torarica. The Sanford brothers confronted Byam and his cronies – 'did very insolently spit in the face of authority'. His rule, they proclaimed, was 'usurpt', 'arbitrary and tyrannical'. Did not the settlers have rights as Englishmen under Magna Carta? they asked, before leaving the meeting with a call for revolt. Byam responded by 'garrisoning his house' and putting 'parties in boats upon the river'.

At this point the Sanford faction took fright, and decided for their own safety to flee the country. According to a letter written by his neighbour Trefry, Robert Sanford was convinced that Byam was trying to have him poisoned. At first the rebels, now including Mashart, returned from the woods, bribed the captain of an English ship to take them secretly to Jamaica. But the plan miscarried and instead they seized the sloop of a local Dutch resident, which was anchored near Jewish Savannah. Their first move was to procure arms to defend their 'prize'.

Byam, hearing report of this, was convinced that the rebels intended to block the river and 'seize my person'. Militia members in canoes were ordered to surround the vessel and demand its surrender. Although the twelve men on board were for a while 'all in a warlike posture', they surrendered as reinforcements loyal to Byam arrived. The Sanfords and their comrades were brought back in chains and dumped in Torarica's gaol.

But Robert Sanford was not done yet. He was a gifted orator and soon all Torarica was gathering to hear him declaim Byam from the window of his prison cell, or as Byam put it, he 'vomited such pickled language as exceeded the rhetoric of Billingsgate.' Byam was forced to remove the Sanfords to a vessel anchored in the river. From there Robert and his brother were deported to Barbados, and their possessions in Suriname seized as payment of a swiftly imposed fine.

Byam now moved against his other critics. According to Sanford's later complaint to London, all those who 'disputed Byam's authority' were also seized, 'many asleep in the beds', by 'parties of musketeers', then clapped in irons and given a rudimentary court martial. Then, still protesting their innocence, they were heavily fined and deported.

The Sanfords' complaint was heard in London in 1663, put aside, picked up again, then disappears from the surviving record. In 1665 Robert Sanford was in Barbados, still 'stirring trouble'. Worse was to come in Suriname for the colony's social fabric, but clearly the halcyon days of the 1650s, with Royalist and Roundhead factions united in shared hard work, effective independence, struggle and success, were over.

William Scot arrived in Suriname on the run. His father was the notorious Thomas Scot, architect of Cromwell's secret services. Thomas had established networks on the continent and in foreign courts, devised codes and recruited cryptographers, set up agents and safe houses, as well as infiltrating Royalist schemes at home – such as Willoughby's Booth's Uprising plot. A fervent believer in the 'Old Cause', he had been amongst those ransacking Lambeth Palace for any sign of popery and was responsible for the outrage of the bones of sixteenth-century Anglican archbishop Matthew Parker being dug up and thrown on a rubbish heap. Like George Marten's brother Henry, Thomas Scot had been an enthusiastic signer of King Charles I's death warrant.

Thomas Scot fell out with Cromwell over the establishment of the Protectorate and was replaced as head of the secret services by John Thurloe. But Scot was reinstated after the fall of Richard Cromwell. A noted womaniser, he kept a long-term mistress with whom he had three daughters, to add to the six other children he had with his first and second wives.

His son William, although trained as a lawyer, through the help of his father secured a job at the Post Office, closely linked at that time to the secret services. During the mid-1650s he had worked for his father's successor Thurloe on spying missions in France. Like his father, he acquired a reputation as a ladies' man, as well as one for improvidence, on several occasions requiring urgent financial assistance.

By the end of 1659, Thomas Scot was riding high; he was made *Custos Rotulorum* (keeper of the rolls) of Westminster and secretary of state. He was among those sent to greet General George Monck at Leicester, but totally misread the way the wind was blowing. As late as April 1660, with the return of the King only weeks away, he made a defiant speech in the Commons, confessing his part in the execution of Charles I and declaring, 'I do not repent of any thing I have done; if it were to do, I could do it again.'

As a regicide, Thomas Scot found his name missing from the Act of Oblivion and, realising the danger at last, fled abroad. But his ship was captured by pirates who, having taken everything of value, dumped him on the Hampshire coast. With the help of sympathisers, he tried again, this time reaching Flanders in the Spanish Netherlands (modern Belgium). But now, however, the Low Countries were awash with Royalist agents and bounty hunters, looking to bring in or simply assassinate the fled regicides. He was spotted, but gave his pursuers the slip thanks to a local friend, the former Spanish ambassador to England. Then the government in London announced that those who gave themselves up and asked for clemency might suffer fines, confiscations or exile, but their lives would be spared. So on 12 July Scot was persuaded to return to England and hand himself over.

He was straight away committed to the Tower and, along with twenty-eight other prisoners, including Henry Marten, was brought to trial on 10 October. For Scot, the promise of clemency proved hollow and he was sentenced to death. The morning he was to die, he received a visit from his wife, a daughter and two sons. It is not known if William was one of them, but it is unlikely. They found him contemptuous of his accusers and unbowed, making the family promise not to beg, as was customary, for his body to be spared the usual mutilations reserved for traitors. On the scaffold on 17 October 1660, and facing the appalling horror of being hanged, drawn and quartered, he remained defiant. Before his final speech was cut short by the sheriff, he declared, 'I cannot, no, I cannot desert the cause.'

Meanwhile his son William had become a wanted man. An arrest warrant was issued which included an allegation that he had stolen £1,000 from the postal service. William slipped away to Holland, where he seems to have got involved with other exiled Parliamentarians, securing arms and plotting opposition to the returned King. But the experience of his father and other exiles who had been snatched back to England soon persuaded him to put more distance between himself and home. Two of the regicides had escaped to New England, but Scot had a brother in

Suriname, a Major Richard, who had recently married the daughter of Nonconformist preacher John Oxenbridge. It was therefore to Willoughbyland that he now fled.

William Scot does not seem to have shared his father's staunch convictions. There are hints that even before the Restoration he was hedging his bets, offering to work for the Royalists from inside his father's intelligence organisation. (Another brother of his, Thomas, betrayed a Roundhead plot in Ireland, and thereby saved his skin.) After the grisly killing of his father, William was bent on self-preservation. Part of his strategy was to retreat out of reach, he hoped, of Charles's agents, but he may also have been looking to start negotiations, from a safe distance, for his acceptance by the new authorities as a double agent. He was, in theory, well placed to infiltrate and thereby spy for the English government on two threats: the Roundhead exiles and the Dutch. With his father's property forfeited by the treason conviction, there was also a pressing need for him to work for anyone who would pay.

For operators like William, who had a reputation as a great talker and prodigious spendthrift on women and wine, money was the bottom line. Among most of his espionage fraternity, there seems to have been little other motivation – spies turned double or even triple agent depending on the reward available. Perhaps understandably, therefore, it was not the policy of Whitehall to leave only one agent in the field: spies would be spied on in turn. No one was to be trusted.

By now Suriname had been thoroughly infected by the secrecy, materialism and complicated disloyalties that were endemic to the Restoration. Robert Sanford had complained that 'no society or scarce family [was] found empty of an informer.' Byam, through his own agents, kept a close watch on William Scot, noting that he consorted with the republican faction in Willoughbyland, whom Byam called 'the brethren'. His fear was that this party, if it could dominate the colony, might declare for the vanquished Parliamentary cause, just as Barbados had declared for the executed King. Byam also knew that Scot had links with the Dutch, who coveted England's rich American territories. Yet Byam was unable to establish exactly for whom Scot was working. Perhaps, as Willoughby had famously done during the Civil War, he had changed sides and was in Suriname as an agent of the proprietor or the King, checking up on the governor after the messy Sanford affair?

And still Willoughby, the proprietor, did not come. In August 1663 he finally reached Barbados, the centre of his new demesne, but for the rest of the year he involved himself in placating the uppity Barbados dons, and in an attempted purchase and settlement of St Lucia. In the meantime, Willoughbyland remained a swamp of confusion and conflict.

Eleven

APHRA BEHN, AGENT 160

'The Poetess too, they say, has Spies abroad.'

APHRA BEHN, PROLOGUE TO *FORC'D MARRIAGE*

'And all my kisses on thy balmy lips as sweet,
As are the breezes breath'd amidst the groves
Of ripening spices on the height of day:
As vigorous too.'

APHRA BEHN, *ABDELAZAR*

Into this volatile situation came twenty-three-year-old
Aphra Behn. Aphra (also known as Astrea or Eafrey)
Johnson, as she then was, was born in 1640, the daughter
of a barber and a wet-nurse. Reportedly a garrulous and
insubordinate child, she grew up in Kent, then gentry-
dominated and surprisingly isolated. As a young woman she
was described as 'of a generous and open temper, something
passionate'. Tall, with bright eyes and flowing brown hair,
she was considered witty and beautiful. A friend would later
write that 'as she was the mistress of uncommon charms of

Aphra Behn, alias Agent 160, sketched by George Scharf from a portrait believed to be lost.

body as well as mind, she gave infinite raging desires.' But, although at twenty-three she was at prime marrying age, she was dowry-less.

Aphra Behn would later become one of the most successful dramatists of the Restoration period, writing nearly twenty plays as well as novellas, poetry and translations. Daniel Defoe would consider her to be among 'the giants of wit and sense' of her age. During the 1670s, only Dryden had more plays performed in London. There was even talk of making her a 'female laureate'. Her reputation plummeted in the 200 years after her death in 1689, critics calling her 'a reproach to her womanhood and a disgrace even to the licentious age in which she lived', but she was rehabilitated in the twentieth century and celebrated for being the first Englishwoman to make her living through writing. Virginia Woolf, in *A Room of One's Own*, describes Behn as 'shady and amorous . . . a middle-class woman with all the plebeian virtues of humour, vitality and courage', and declares, 'All women together ought to let flowers fall upon the tomb of Aphra Behn, for it was she who earned them the right to speak their minds.'

Behn's most successful play was *The Rover*, about a group of exiled Cavaliers in Madrid, but her masterpiece was the story – sometimes called the first English psychological novel – *Oroonoko*, published in 1688 but set in Suriname at the time of her visit in 1663–4. Like almost everything written about the area from Ralegh onwards, it contains substantial elements of romance and fantasy – in this case showing the influence on Behn of the hugely popular heroic historical epics by Seigneur de La Calprenède – but it also constitutes one of the most vivid and detailed first-hand accounts we have of Willoughbyland during its brief existence.

Just as Ralegh was accused of making up his 1595 expedition to Guiana while 'skulking in Cornwall', for many years a debate was held as to whether Aphra Behn actually visited Suriname, or whether instead she garnered information about it from George Warren's book, or other sources circulating in London in the 1660s. This latter view was put forward in a paper published in 1913. However, since then letters – from William Byam and John Trefry – have come to light that appear to place her in Suriname in 1663–4.

In *Oroonoko*, the first-person narrator, whom the reader is encouraged to see as the real historical Aphra Behn, claims to be an 'eye-witness' to the colony. And certainly much of the content of the story supports this claim, as the book contains precise and accurate details of everything from topography to slave prices to indigenous people, as well as local words, uncommon or even unheard in England: 'cat-o'-nine-tails' 'backerary', 'osenbrigs', 'hamaca', 'savan', 'pickaninnies', 'paddle', 'punch'. This is very different from her other works set abroad, in France or Spain for example, where she never provides even the most rudimentary local colour. Furthermore, all the Europeans named in *Oroonoko* – including John Trefry, George Marten and William Byam – were, as we have seen, real people who were there. Thus the overwhelming consensus amongst Behn scholars and biographers is: yes, she was in Suriname.

It has been variously suggested that Behn was amorously connected to Willoughby or someone else already out there, that she was in search of a husband or that she was joining a 'kinsman' (who appears in a brief episode in her account). The narrator of *Oroonoko* claims that she was accompanying her father who had been made lieutenant general of the colony, but this is the most unlikely explanation of all, as there is no record of such an appointment. By some way the most convincing answer, however, is that she was sent there as a spy.

There is evidence that Behn spied or at least acted as a courier and copyist for the Royalists in Europe before the Restoration. Her foster brother was, like Willoughby, a member of the Sealed Knot conspiracy. She seems to have met the influential courtier Thomas Killigrew, who was in exile with Charles II in the Spanish Netherlands and involved with intelligence. Killigrew was friends with Willoughby and had sons with plantations in the West Indies. It was probably through him that Behn was later employed as a Royalist spy in Flanders in 1666. Then, as most likely in Suriname, her code names were variously 'Astrea' or 'Agent 160'.

So who sent her? It might have been Clarendon, Charles II's lord chancellor who had had his son appointed joint proprietor with Willoughby. Or was it the King himself? On Behn's return from the colony, she had an audience with Charles II, to give him 'An account of his Affairs there'. Or maybe it was Willoughby, to whom she was distantly related, or one of his agents? Perhaps Willoughby felt that an eye needed to be kept on the newly autocratic Byam after the Sanford business. Or more generally to report back, including a remit to discover if the fears of a union between the Indians and recently arrived slaves from Africa were justified.

It is likely that the brief from any of these men would have included the order to contact William Scot, who, on later evidence, would almost certainly have been looking to put out feelers to switch sides and turn double agent. We know that she succeeded in this, with somewhat unexpected consequences.

Behn travelled with her mother, her sister, her 'maid of much courage' and her younger brother, leaving England around the beginning of May 1663. The journey probably lasted between six and nine weeks. (Renatus Enys reported the duration of his 'fair voyage' to Suriname as nine weeks, although Ralegh had done it in six.) According to Behn's narrator, her father died at sea and was heaved overboard in the usual fashion. This may have been true, as Behn's actual father died sometime between 1662 and 1664. More likely, it was a cover story to explain her arrival in Suriname without a male guardian. The narrator of *Oroonoko* certainly seems strangely unmoved by the supposedly recent loss of her father.

Their ship, then, reached its destination in around July 1663. The sea off the Suriname river was brown with sediment and the coastline swampy, but as ever it was a scene of dolphins and flocks of brightly coloured birdlife. At the mouth of the river – on 'Byam's Pointe' – stood a small wooden fort and a handful of huts, but their vessel headed upstream, sticking to the left-hand side to avoid the shoals. After about fifteen miles, they reached Paramaribo, where a larger, though still wooden-walled, fort guarded the river, and a number of buildings – all of cedar – clustered nearby. After a stop, the ship continued upstream.

On the banks, the passengers would have seen vegetation richer and thicker than anything they had ever come across. No doubt, like another traveller, they would have enjoyed the spicy aromas of the tropical trees, 'the Sense of Smelling which may, at any time, enjoy a full delight amongst the Woods, which disperse their Aromatick Odours a good distance from the Land, to the no little pleasure of the Sea-tired Passengers.' Occasionally, when the ground was higher, there were open fields, but mostly both sides were 'Woody, unless here and there a plantation be open to it'. They would have stopped for refreshments, or to spend the night at various plantations, each with their own landing stage and boats.

By now the river had become more winding. As George Warren wrote, the waterway took 'so perfect a Meander, that in a matter of fifteen Leagues' sailing, a ship steers all points of the Compass'. It was as if it were designed to make incomers lose their bearings. And if anyone asked the source of the river, they would receive the disconcerting answer that it 'continues as far as hath been discover'd'. On a map drawn around 1667, the Suriname river simply stops at a place called Sarah's Creek. George Warren explains that the river was settled for thirty leagues, but beyond that there were falls every five or six leagues, 'for ought is known'.

At Torarica it is likely that the passengers would have switched to a smaller boat to press on upstream, past Byam's main plantation on the left bank into the region of Jewish Savannah, where the sandy soil meant fewer large trees and more open land. Another fifteen miles or so further up the main branch of the river stood Parham Hill, Willoughby's chief plantation in the colony, but Behn's destination was down a small tributary a couple of miles shy of Parham Hill: St John's Hill, one of the three plantations owned by Sir Robert Harley, Willoughby's fellow Royalist plotter and friend (for the moment), and chancellor of Barbados. Harley seems to have recently purchased the plantation from William Byam, and had there a 'very thriving stock of cattle'.

According to Behn's narrator, St John's Hill boasted the finest house in the colony, standing on a 'vast Rock of white

Marble' on the edge of the river. Today, pieces of white quartz-like rock can still be found in the region of the site, now long returned to jungle. From the river came the noise of the waves washing against the foot of the rock, making the 'softest Murmurs and Purlings in the World'. On the opposite bank could be seen a blaze of colour from flowers of many different hues, forever blooming 'every day and hour new' and behind them 'lofty trees of a thousand rare forms', a view 'the most ravishing that fancy can create'. Leading from the house to the river was a long grove of citrus trees that gave shelter from the sun, which together with the cool breeze from the water made it the most delightful place in 'the whole Globe of the world', superior even to the finest gardens of 'boasted Italy'.

Like any unfamiliar visitor to Suriname today, Behn seems to have been struck with wonder and awe at the stunning natural beauty and occasional strangeness of the place. All things, her narrator pronounces, 'by nature there are rare, delightful and wonderful.' She loved the exotic fragrances of nutmeg, citrus and balsam that wafted from the trees. Soon, she was taking 'great delight' in 'going in search of divers wonderful and strange things that Country afford.' She was amazed at the marmosets 'of a marvellous and delicate shape, [with] Face and hands like an human creature'; 'great parrots, Muckaws, and a thousand other birds and beasts of wonderful and surprising forms, shapes and colours'; 'Prodigious snakes, of which there are some threescore Yards in length'; and rare butterflies, 'of amazing forms and colours . . . some as big as my fist, some less: and all of various excellencies, such as art cannot imitate'.

George Warren described Willoughbyland as 'a brave Country . . . no place is more accommodate: whether we regards health, a luxuriant Soyle, or kind women.' Aphra Behn seems to have agreed. Not only was it of 'vast Extent', reaching 'one way as far as China, and another to Peru' as the narrator of *Oroonoko* informs us, it also afforded 'all things for Beauty and Use' and enjoyed 'eternal spring, always the very Months of April, May and June.'

Nature was not always benign. Behn's narrator complains of the scorching heat of the sun, and describes herself as 'very sickly, and apt to fall into Fits of dangerous Illness.' Like others, she notes the danger of 'Tigers' in the jungle, and 'numb eels' in the rivers.

Most threatening to the vision of Arcadia, though, were the people of the colony.

Behn clearly made good friends, including George Marten, described in *Oroonoko* as 'so brave a man . . . wise and eloquent; [who] from the fineness of his parts, bore a great sway over the hearts of all the colony' and John Trefry, Willoughby's overseer at Parham Hill, 'a man of great wit and fine learning', 'naturally amourous', 'a warm and agreeable companion'. They were, however, the exception:

the lower-class whites – tradesmen, and indentured servants, called here 'Slaves for four years' – were all 'overtaken in drink', and the planters divided by feuds, with many antagonistic to Willoughby. The ruling council, Behn's narrator declares, were 'such notorious Villains as Newgate never transported . . . at the council table would Contradict and Fight with one another, and Swear so bloodily that 'twas terrible to hear, and see 'em.' (In a late play, *The Widow Ranter*, Behn has a character comment on similar colonial upstarts in Virginia: 'Transported criminals who having acquired great estates, are now become your Honour and Rightful Worshipful, and possess all places of authority.')

Apart from the feuds and personality clashes endemic to any small, isolated community, clearly the Restoration had sharpened divisions within the ruling elite. What is striking, though, is the company that Behn kept during her stay in Willoughbyland. She was an ardent Royalist – she has her hero Oroonoko comment on the 'deplorable death' of Charles I – and her works are consistent in portraying virtuous Royalists and put-upon nobles who are opposed by petty and evil republicans/Parliamentarians. Yet William Byam and his deputy James Banister, both actual Royalists, are portrayed in *Oroonoko* as malicious, licentious and sadistic. Byam, possibly the most fervent Royalist in the colony, is to Behn 'the most fawning fair-tongu'd fellow in the world . . . not fit to be mentioned with the worst of

157

slaves.' Banister is 'a wild Irishman . . . a fellow of absolute barbarity, and fit to execute any villainy.' In contrast, George Marten, whose brother Henry was one of the most virulent opponents of the King during the 1640s and, like William Scot's father, a regicide, is shown to be reasonable, open-minded and fair, 'a man of great gallantry wit and goodness'. George Marten was certainly seen to be one of the Parliamentary 'brethren', so why did he, unlike the committed Royalists, come in for praise from Aphra Behn?

Personalities, of course, can transcend politics, and events – such as depicted in *Oroonoko* – often show people in surprising lights. Nevertheless, a revealing letter from William Byam to friends in Barbados points to another explanation. In it, Byam makes clear that a love affair, or at least a deep attachment, had come about between Aphra Behn and the man she was sent to spy on – the silver-tongued womaniser William Scot, married and middle-aged though he was. Byam describes it as a 'sympathetical passion' and by the end of the year the relationship had clearly become common gossip in the colony. Scot, we learn, later 'resolved to espouse all distress or felicities of fortune' with Aphra. This might well have drawn Aphra Behn, despite her own politics, into Scot's republican circle, which would have included George Marten. Marten, like his brother, had a reputation as a lover of fine wines, the debts for which would more than once nearly be the ruin of him. He had written to his brother from Barbados requesting 'three or four dozen glass bottles of excellent Canary that I may not in drinking your health lose my own, which is in great danger, [for] I do so often remember you in bad wine.' Both William Scot and Aphra Behn were, or would become, enthusiastic tipplers. It is easy to imagine the three becoming intimately intoxicated on a warm Suriname night.

Behn's first play, *The Young King*, which she wrote while in Suriname, includes a character who is seen having his first (albeit drugged) taste of wine, which has the instant effect of making his lover even more attractive:

> Methinks my Soul is grown more gay and vigorous;
> What I've drank, has deifi'd thee more,
> Heightens the pleasures which I take to gaze on thee,
> And sends a thousand strange uneasie Joys,
> That play about my Heart, and more transport me.

Three years later, Behn would be sent as a secret agent to Europe to 'bring in' William Scot, by then working as an agent for the Dutch. The surviving record of their relationship at that time gives more than a few hints of ongoing romantic intimacy. When he is away, she is full of doubts, calling him a 'rogue'. But his presence wins her over, causing her to write, 'I believe him in all things.' As it would turn out, their relationship would be of huge consequence for the future of Willoughbyland.

Twelve

SUGAR, SLAVERY AND *OROONOKO*

'Those who talk much of a new world of the
Indies say more than they ofttimes know.'
JAMAICAN PLANTOCRAT PETER BECKFORD, 1672

If Aphra Behn's primary role was to watch William Scot,
then she was almost certainly also charged with reporting
on all aspects of the colony, including its indigenous people,
the 'Indians'.

Ralegh's dream of a grand alliance between the English and
the 'Incas' against mutual enemy Spain seems, by this time, to
have been forgotten. Instead English views on the indigenous
peoples of Suriname and the islands, where significant
populations still existed in Dominica, St Vincent, Grenada
and St Lucia, had evolved into a split between those who
considered them as noble, a people unspoilt by the degraded
morals and artificial tastes of Europe, and those who regarded
them as vicious cannibals to be displaced or destroyed.

(Willoughby's instructions on taking up governorship of the Caribbees were to 'treat with the natives . . . or if injurious or contumacious, to persecute them with fire and sword.') George Warren, in his short account of Suriname, takes both positions, describing the 'Indians' as a 'happy people as to this world . . . nature with little toil providing all things' and 'naturally docile and ingenious', but also treacherous, barbaric and cruel.

The narrator of *Oroonoko* definitely tends towards the former view, with her description of the indigenous people owing much to the attitude of widely read sixteenth-century French essayist Michel de Montaigne's 'Of Cannibals'. Montaigne contrasts the 'useful and natural virtues' of the indigenous Brazilians he met in France, with the degeneracy and corruption of his own people. The 'Cannibals' live in purity and 'original simplicity', 'the very words that signify lying, treachery, dissimulation, avarice, envy, detraction, pardon never heard of.'

The indigenous people of Willoughbyland are described in *Oroonoko* as not only 'finely shap'd', but also blessed with 'a natural justice, which knows no fraud; they understand no vice, or cunning, but when they are taught by the white men . . . these people represented to me an absolute idea of the first State of Innocence'. Indeed there are plenty of references to man's prelapsarian state: their small coverings are like 'Adam and Eve did the fig-leaves'. Their modesty is 'like our first Parents before the Fall'.

She is less consistent, however, when describing their relations with the English settlers. Near the beginning of the story, we are told how they traded food for 'very small and unvaluable trifles' with whites, with whom they live 'in perfect Tranquillity'. Yet later she recounts how, 'About this time we were in many mortal Fears, about some disputes the English had with the Indians; so that we could scarce trust our selves, without great Numbers, to go to any Indian towns, or place, where they abode; for fear they should fall upon us.'

Nevertheless, together with her maid, her brother and other companions, the narrator of *Oroonoko* journeys upriver by canoe for eight days in order to visit a remote indigenous village, where the inhabitants have never before seen white people. When they reach it, they land and make their way towards the settlement. In the distance they see a group dancing, while others are collecting water from the river and going about different household tasks. Then they are spotted and 'they set up a loud cry, that frighted us at first; we thought it had been for those that should kill us, but it seems it was of wonder and amazement.'

Behn paints the scene for her reader with great skill. The 'Indians' were all 'naked', save for the 'beads, bits of tin . . . and any shining trinket' hanging from pierced ears, noses and lips, while 'we were dressed very glittering and rich . . . My own hair was cut short, and I had a Taffaty

Indigenous Surinamese depicted in a book published during the period of Dutch rule. An English visitor in the 1660s commented that they were 'frequent and excessive' in 'confused dancing.'

cap, with black feathers on my head.' She is also wearing petticoats, shoes, stockings and garters lined with silver lace. Her brother is similarly heavily laden in a worsted suit 'with silver loops and buttons, and abundance of green ribbon'. As might be expected in the blazing heat, this was all 'infinitely surprising to them'.

For a few moments the two groups stare at each other. Then the narrator and her brother advance and offer their hands, which the Indians take, calling to their fellows to come out and see the strange arrivals. Soon the 'Indians' are 'laying their Hands upon all the Features of our Faces, feeling our Breasts and Arms, taking up one Petticoat, then wondering to see another; admiring our Shoes and Stockings, but more our Garters.' The last the narrator hands over as gifts and in return receives a present of brightly coloured feathers. (Aphra Behn would, indeed, bring some beautiful feathers back to England.) The English pair call to their companions to join them, including an 'Indian trader' who acts as interpreter. Then they are all treated to a meal, served on large leaves, of 'Venison and Buffelo': 'very good, but too high season'd with Pepper'. According to Behn's narrator, this fraternisation led to 'so good an understanding between the Indians and the English, that there were no more Fears or Heartburnings during our stay.'

On their return downriver, the group encounter different-looking 'Indians' of 'strange Aspects', dressed in 'Skins of a strange beast'. It turns out they had come from the distant mountains, and most excitingly, they are carrying in small bags a quantity of gold dust. Clearly the El Dorado fantasy is still alive and well in Willoughbyland. The Indians are taken to Parham Hill to await the arrival of the governor, who is sent some of the gold.

For all this, however, the most striking thing about the colony for Aphra Behn was not its creatures, nor gold, nor 'Indians', but African slavery, which became, of course, the principal inspiration for her *Oroonoko*.

*

Throughout the West Indies, the establishment and expansion of the sugar industry, with its huge demand for labour, brought in its wake an exponential increase in the importation of enslaved Africans. In both, Barbados had led the way for the English colonies, and as early as 1653 had a slave population of 20,000, supplied in the main by Dutch traders. As the other English islands – St Kitts, Antigua, Nevis, Montserrat, Jamaica – adopted the Barbados plantation model over the following decades, so they too converted their labour force from freemen, or indentured white servants, to enslaved Africans.

In Willoughbyland, it is likely that some of the incomers from Barbados in the 1650s brought black slaves with their households, although there is no reference to them from that time. There is an intriguing note in Renatus Enys's report to London on the colony, compiled in around September 1663. He writes, 'Were the planters supplied with negroes, the strength and sinews of this western world, they would advance their fortunes and his Majesty's customs.' The reason for the lack of supply, he assumes, is that 'eminent Barbadians' were deliberately keeping the imported slaves for themselves in an effort to retard the development of Suriname as a rival sugar colony. There are vague references to 'Negroes' in a pamphlet about the colony published in 1662. But the implication of Enys's comment is that in late 1663, there were only a few enslaved Africans working in Willoughbyland. This was about to change.

Soon after his Restoration in 1660, Charles II had established a new company, the Royal Adventurers, to run the Africa trade, with his brother the Duke of York (later James II) as president. Much of the capital came from members of the court. The emphasis was on gold, with slaves of minor importance. It was not a success, partly because of impediment from the Dutch on the West Africa coast where they claimed a monopoly, and in January 1663 a new charter was issued for the Royal Adventurers. This was an altogether more determined effort: shareholders now included the King himself, as well as the Duke of York, who invested £2,000, the Queen and the Queen Mother, as well as many other notables, including John Locke and Samuel Pepys. And the emphasis was now firmly on the slave trade, in which the company was granted a monopoly to supply the English Caribbean. This company, then, can be seen as a turning point: the moment when slavery in the English empire was given official sanction and backing. Now England was determined to control and profit from the sale of slaves to its colonies, rather than lose out to the Dutch.

The first step was to restore the English forts on the coast of West Africa and take back those seized by the Dutch or Swedes; £300,000 was spent on this endeavour. The initial two ships sent out to Guinea for slaves were, fittingly, the

Charles and the *James*. In all, forty ships set sail in the first year. Enslaved Africans were branded 'DY' for the Duke of York. The governor of the fledgling colony of Jamaica was promised 300; Willoughby in Barbados was told he could expect 3,000 delivered each year. The company was as good as its word: in the seven months after August 1663, a total of 3,075 enslaved Africans was landed there.

In each territory, the company appointed an agent to handle the sale, collect payment, and ensure that no unlicensed traders could operate. In Suriname, somewhat inevitably, this position went to William Byam.

On 27 January 1664, an employee of Sir Robert Harley called William Yearworth, who was looking after one of his plantations in the Jewish Savannah region, reported to his master that three days before, 'A guinea man arrived here in this river . . . She has 130 nigroes on board.' This may not have been the very first major shipment to arrive, but certainly it was quickly followed by many more. Aphra Behn, who left Suriname soon afterwards, baldly stated in *Oroonoko*, 'Those then whom we make use of to work in our plantations of sugar, are negro's, black-slaves altogether; which are transported thither.' She also describes the 'Houses of the slaves' at Parham Hill as 'like a little town'. John Oxenbridge, who likely wrote his account of Suriname in late 1665, pointed out that 'for help with in labour, you may more easily than in cold Countries procure

*Slaves arriving in Suriname. Official sanction for the slave trade from
Charles II saw sudden large imports after 1663.*

and maintain heathen bond-servants, (Blacks or other)'.
Indeed, by 1667, there appear to have been as many as 3,000
enslaved Africans in the colony.

Slavery poisoned everything. Antoine Biet, the French
priest who had visited Willoughbyland in 1653 and been
most impressed, had proceeded to Barbados, which had
already converted to a racialised slave society. He was

appalled by what he found: not only by the vicious cruelty with which the white population kept the black half of the population suppressed and in miserable degradation, but also by the drunken and decadent lifestyles of the planters, waited on hand and foot and freed from the rigours of work in the field. As well as moral sickness, there was the physical sickness too, as the slave ships had brought from Africa yellow fever mosquitoes that killed thousands of Europeans who had no immunity.

Now, ten years later, Willoughbyland was following the same dismal path. It was the final end of Ralegh's vision of a white settler community, absorbing surplus English population and giving anyone who wanted it a new start. Instead, the colony would be a place of horror and humiliation for those Africans forcibly removed there and a place of fear and viciousness for the whites.

For the enslaved Africans, the 'Middle Crossing' itself was an almost unimaginable torment. William Yearworth, who wrote to Harley to tell him of the arrival of the slave ship, added the information that the voyage across the ocean had claimed the lives of fifty-four out of the original complement of 180 people, some thirty per cent. This was not unusual: the average was about a quarter. Unless the shipment was atypical, the biggest killer was simple thirst. Vessels never carried enough water for even the minimum necessary consumption per head.

George Warren, complimentary about much of what he saw in Suriname in the mid-1660s, makes an exception when he turns to write 'Of the Negroes, Or Slaves'. The survivors of the Middle Passage, he reports, were 'sold like Dogs' and valued for nothing but their labour, 'which they perform all the Week with the severest usages for the slightest fault.' While the newly-rich sugar planters built lavish mansions and gorged themselves on vast quantities of food and alcohol, no effort was made to house or clothe the slaves properly. They had to grow their own food, 'unless perhaps once or twice a year, their Masters vouchsafe them, as a great favour, a little rotten Salt-fish.' Their 'wretched miseries', Warren writes, often drove them to attempt escape, and if recaptured alive they were subjected to 'the most exquisite tortures'. Many, he says, preferred death to 'that indeed unequalled slavery'.

Behn writes of the constant atmosphere of terror that this tyranny and cruelty engendered in everyone, with the white people in fear of 'Mutinies – which is very fatal sometimes in those colonies, that abound so with Slaves.' Behn's novel is at heart a vivid depiction of this situation.

After the narrator of *Oroonoko* has introduced herself as an 'eye-witness' to the main part of the story, and given a brief description of Suriname, the action begins in 'Coromantien', West Africa. This was a contemporary European term for the region that is now Ghana, derived from the name of a fortified English trading station on the Gold Coast. Behn's narrator explains that it 'was one of those places in which they found the most advantageous Trading for slaves . . . for that nation is very war-like and brave; and having a continual campaign, being always in hostility with one neighbouring prince or another, they had the fortune to take a great many captives; for all they took in battle, were sold as slaves.' All people shipped from the region – who would have been mainly Ashanti and Fanti, and other Akan (or Twi) speakers – were called Cormantines or Cormantees by European slave traders, and they gained a reputation for their intelligence, skills as carpenters and blacksmiths and strength as workers in general. This made them highly prized, but they were also feared for their rebelliousness.

The 'King of Coramantien', Behn's narrator explains, is a very old man, all of whose sons have been killed in battle. He has a seventeen-year-old grandson, though, the eponymous hero, Oroonoko. The young man's face is 'a perfect ebony', his eyes piercing, his nose 'Roman, instead of African and flat' and his mouth 'has the finest shape that could be seen; far from those great turn'd lips, which are so natural to the rest of the Negroes.' He has been tutored by a Frenchman in 'morals, language and science', as well as learning English and Spanish from trading on the coast, and he is witty, charming, courageous, with an altogether 'great and just character'.

He has been away fighting, and when he returns he meets Imoinda, 'the most beautiful that ever had been seen'. They fall in love and pledge themselves to one another, but then she is spotted by the King, who orders her to join his harem. Before the King can sleep with her, Oroonoko breaks in and they consummate their love. When this is discovered, the King discards Imoinda, selling her into slavery, although he tells Oroonoko that she has met the less humiliating fate of execution.

Shortly afterwards Oroonoko himself is tricked into slavery by an English trader and shipped to Suriname. There – after a journey on which many of the Africans die, like that described by Yearworth – he is renamed 'Caesar' and sold to Willoughby's agent at Parham Hill, John Trefry, the 'young Cornish gentleman . . . of great wit and learning'. Trefry is astonished by Oroonoko's education and nobility and promises to return him to his own country.

Meanwhile, the narrator has arrived in Suriname a little before this with her family and they are lodged at the nearby plantation of St John's Hill. She befriends the African prince, as does George Marten. Oroonoko discovers that by a happy coincidence Imoinda is also at Parham Hill. They are reunited and she becomes pregnant.

This spurs Oroonoko to press harder for his freedom, lest their child be born a slave. He offers gold and 'a vast quantity of slaves' in return for his and his family's freedom, but Trefry, although extremely sympathetic, reluctantly insists that such a decision has to wait for the arrival of Willoughby. Fed up with the delay, Oroonoko leads a rebellion of the slaves, who head for the sea in the hope of a vessel to carry them home. While the narrator and other women flee down the river, fearing 'he would come down and cut all our throats', Byam and the colony's 600-strong militia go in pursuit and there is a battle. Byam is hit by a poisoned arrow fired by Imoinda but saved by his 'Indian mistress' who sucks out the poison. Then Oroonoko's followers desert him. Eventually Byam persuades him to surrender, promising in writing to give him and his family their freedom.

But Byam betrays him. Oroonoko is seized, and whipped almost to death. Then 'Indian pepper' is rubbed into his wounds. The narrator hears of this on her way downriver and is appalled: 'I had authority and interest enough there,' she declares, 'had I suspected any such thing, to have prevented it.' On the river she meets George Marten who as 'a friend of Caesar, resented this false dealing with him very much.' They return together upriver, and take Oroonoko to Parham Hill, where they give him a 'healing bath, to rid him of his pepper, and order a surgeon to anoint him with healing balm.' Oroonoko promises to revenge himself on Byam and not even the advice of George Marten, for whom Oroonoko has 'a great respect . . . like that of a parent', can dissuade him.

When Byam hears of Oroonoko's recovery, he calls together
the 'notorious villains' of his council, who unanimously
decide that Oroonoko must be made an example of to 'all
the Negroes, to fright 'em from daring to threaten their
betters.' Trefry then declares that Byam's writ does not run
at Parham Hill and sets a guard at the plantation's riverside
landing. In the meantime, though, Oroonoko takes Imoinda
into the woods, and with her consent kills her, so that she
and their child when it is born shan't be left to his enemies.
But having committed the deed, he is overcome with grief,
so when eight days later he is found by a search party, he has
only strength enough to mutilate himself, cutting a piece off
his throat and opening up his stomach, before once again he
is carried back to Parham Hill and treated by the surgeon.
Above all, he wants to die, and the doctor assures him he
will. 'We were all (but Caesar) afflicted by this news,' the
narrator reports, 'and the sight was gashly.'

It is all too much for the narrator, who takes herself
off downriver to George Marten's plantation, having been
assured that Oroonoko would be given the best care. But
while she is away, Byam sends Trefry on an errand upriver,
and in his absence Byam's deputy Banister arrives, seizes
Oroonoko, and returns him to the whipping post of his
previous punishment. There, Oroonoko is castrated, then
gradually cut into pieces – ears, nose, arms – which are
thrown into a fire in front of him. All the time he smokes

OROONOKO:

OR, THE

Royal Slave.

A TRUE

HISTORY.

By Mrs. *A. BEHN.*

LONDON,

Printed for *Will. Canning,* at his Shop in
the *Temple-Cloysters.* 1688.

The title page of the first edition of Oroonoko, *with its bold and unusual
declaration that it is 'A True History'.*

a pipe, until 'he gave up the Ghost, without a groan, or a reproach'. He is then cut into quarters, which are despatched to the 'chief plantations'. One is sent to George Marten, 'who refused it; and swore, he had rather see the quarters of Banister, and the Governor himself, than those of Caesar . . . and that he could govern his negroes without terrifying and grieving them with frightful spectacles of a mangled king.' 'Thus died this great man,' the story ends, 'worthy of a better fate, and a more sublime wit than mine to write his Praise.'

Initial sales of *Oroonoko* were disappointing, but the story remained popular thanks to its adaptation for the stage by Thomas Southerne in 1695. Southerne stays fairly faithful to Behn's story, with the exception that he makes Imoinda white. Along with *The Tempest* and *Othello*, Southerne's *Oroonoko* was one of the most popular dramas in the British theatrical repertory of the 1700s.

This brought many readers to the book, which became a seminal text in the sentimental anti-slavery tradition that grew steadily through the eighteenth century. The story was mobilised so successfully by the Abolitionist movement that the play was never performed in slave-trading Liverpool. 'Aphra Behn's contribution to the preparation for the abolitionist movement can scarcely be exaggerated,' writes Hugh Thomas, chronicler of the slave trade. 'She helped to prepare literary people's minds for a change on humanitarian grounds. She was more influential than popes or missionaries.' Certainly, Behn enabled Europeans to understand the concept of enslavement in a way that had not been attempted before. She was also the first European author who tried to render the life lived by sub-Saharan African characters on their own continent, thereby building a bridge of sympathy and understanding over the huge gulf that divided the very different cultures.

However, the book is not entirely condemning of the slave trade as an institution. Behn objected not so much to slavery, but to the enslavement of a prince, whatever his race. The sympathetic characters Trefry and Marten are both slave owners. Indeed, Oroonoko himself is a slave trader; when he first meets Imoinda he presents her with 150 slaves 'in fetters', and he deems enslavement justifiable for those captured in a war. Nonetheless, details of how a slave society operated were little known in England at the end of the seventeenth century, and it is easy to see how the individuality and nobility of the black hero and heroine presented a severe challenge to those who would later defend slavery on grounds of racial inferiority.

Behn gave her novel the subtitle 'A True History', and declared in her Dedicatory Epistle that 'what I have mentioned I have taken care should be truth', a claim she only made for one of her other stories. The novel contains elements of romance and fantasy, of course, just as Ralegh's book did ninety years earlier. But a great deal of it is actually highly plausible.

Many elements of the narrative, big and small, are historically proven: African kings did sell their prisoners of war to European traders; planters in the Caribbean did order slaves in 'lots' and then give them mockingly-heroic classical names such as Caesar; 'Coromantien' Africans like Oroonoko were famously proud and aggressive; slave punishments such as rubbing pepper into the wounds of someone whipped, and various mutilations as suffered by the hero, are well documented in Barbados, Jamaica and elsewhere; like Imoinda and Oroonoko, many enslaved people preferred to die rather than live in servitude.

As we have seen, Byam, Banister, Trefry and Marten – and indeed Behn – are all real people who were in Suriname at the time. Even the attitude of the sympathetically drawn George Marten to his slaves is backed up by records from his time in Barbados, where he seems, unusually, to have let his workers live together as families.

It has been suggested that in giving Oroonoko a 'Roman' nose and thin lips, Behn was 'Europeanising' him for her English readers. In fact, some of the people living in 'Coromantien' were descended from a desert tribe who had migrated south and looked different from other West African tribes. A Frenchman who was there in the 1670s commented on one such man he met 'without the unattractive flat nose or that large mouth that the other blacks have.' And some high-status Africans did, like Oroonoko, have European tutors.

Even the idea of an African king sold into slavery is not as outlandish as it might first appear. In 1675 a large rebellion in Barbados, led by 'Coromantiens', hoped to return to kingship an 'ancient Gold Coast negro' called Cuffee. Three years later 'Escelin, King of Neumon in Guinny' was brought to England having been snatched from West Africa and sold as a slave in Jamaica, then 'redeemed by a merchant in London'.

Indeed, the whole Oroonoko story was vividly brought to life in 1749, when a Fante prince and his companion, previously sold into slavery but ransomed by the British government and received in state in London, attended a performance of Southerne's *Oroonoko*. Affected 'with that generous grief which pure nature always feels', the young prince was so overcome that he was obliged to retire at the end of the fourth act, the *Gentleman's Magazine* reported. His companion remained, but wept the whole time, 'a circumstance that affected the audience yet more than the play, and doubled the tears that were shed for Oroonoko and Imoinda.'

All of this no doubt raises the question as to whether there was a real slave rebellion in Willoughbyland that could have been witnessed by the historical Aphra Behn.

Although the uprising she describes has no specific documented historical counterpart, revolts and desertion were commonplace in the West Indies and Guiana during this period, often led by 'Coromantien' slaves. In fact, while Behn was in Suriname a group of escaped slaves commanded by a 'Coromantien' known as Jermes had established a base in the region of Paramaribo, from which they attacked local plantations. Warren's account, too, indicates that in Suriname rebellions – 'desperate attempts for the recovery of their liberty' – were frequent. Byam himself reports severe problems with 'the insolent disorder of our own Negroes'.

Certainly something of significance happened in late 1663, because shortly afterwards Byam sailed to Barbados to consult with Willoughby, and Trefry was then sacked. Byam also succeeded in throwing Aphra Behn out of the colony, writing to Harley in February 1664, 'I found . . . a full ship freighted and bound for London, on whom I sent off the fair shepherdess . . . with what reluctancy and regret you may well conjecture.' Byam's sarcastic superciliousness, it seems, was undented by the dramatic events of the slave rebellion. Shortly afterwards, on 14 March, another Byam letter tells of the departure of William Scot: 'I need not enlarge but to advise you of the sympathetical passion of the Grand Shepherd Celadon who is fled after Astrea, being resolved to espouse all distress or felicities of fortune with her . . . Truly the brethren are much startled that the

Governor of the Reformation should turn tail on the day of battle.'

Harley would have understood the literary reference to Honoré d'Urfé's *L'Astrée*, a hugely popular story about two lovers, Astrée and Céladon. In addition, Astrea was Behn's pseudonym, and her code name when she later spied in Europe. The initials of Grand Shepherd Celadon are the same as Scot's if you give his first name in Latin (he was, after all, legally-trained): Guglielmus – GSc. Celadon would also be Scot's later alias, and it is possible he was already using it.

Yet Scot did not, could not, follow Behn to England where he was still a wanted man. Instead he landed at Rotterdam in the States of Zeeland. By now, relations between the United Provinces and England were ever worsening, in large part because of the Royal Adventurers' aggressive inroads into the lucrative slave trade at the expense of the Dutch. From Rotterdam, Scot planned his next move. As it turned out, Celadon would see his Astrea again soon.

Thirteen

THE RETURN OF
WILLOUGHBY

'On the sudden
A Roman thought hath struck him'
WILLIAM SHAKESPEARE, *ANTONY AND CLEOPATRA*

'What cares these roarers for
the name of king?'
WILLIAM SHAKESPEARE, *THE TEMPEST*

If these events described by Behn, or at least a version of them, had shaken the colony, then worse was to come. In *Oroonoko*, the narrator deplores the absence of the King's representative, 'every day expected on our shore'. The late Aphra Behn play, *The Widow Ranter*, set in British colonial North America, tells the story of basically good men led astray and vulgar men empowered during the absence of a strong governor. But now, at last, Willoughby, described by Byam as 'Under God being the foundation and essence of this colony', was on his way to Suriname and Willoughbyland would be 'bottomed by royal authority'.

Willoughby landed with his entourage on 18 November 1664, by which stage he was suffering from painful gout. According to Byam, who in his account could not resist comparing this moment to the return of Charles II to England, he arrived back in his fiefdom 'to the inexpressible joy of all the Inhabitants'. A more down-to-earth version explains that 'there was some difference between the inhabitants and his Lordship'. For a number of the planters, it was an opportunity for confrontation, perhaps more.

John Allin was a Londoner who had arrived in Willoughbyland via Barbados in April 1657 and had purchased land. He was clearly an accomplished and hard-working planter, and soon became rich. But according to Byam, this 'heightened strange apprehensions in him, at length making him more for Errantry than planting'. Already known for his independent thinking and 'sarcastical wit', Allin now became addicted to 'swearing, cursing and drunkenness'. He was even accused by Byam of 'entertaining his hours of leisure with Romances and the lives of some bold Romans', which made his brain 'frothy'. In fact, according to another source, Allin was one of a number, a faction – 'several acquaintances' – who refused to acknowledge Willoughby's grant, no doubt because of the threat to property and freedom in Suriname which it represented.

In all, the Restoration had left the colony marked by instability and conflicting, overlapping jurisdictions. Allin's tactful approach was to argue that 'no subject could be a Lord Proprietor as it infringed the liberty of the subject and clipped the wings of the monarchy.'

Perhaps, in addition, the heat and temper of the place had got the better of Allin. This is certainly how Byam wished him to be seen. In 1659, Allin had been tried for blasphemy, and acquitted, but five years later he was again in trouble for swearing and for taking part in a duel with a Captain John Parker, in which Parker had been injured, though not killed. For these offences, he was bound over to appear at sessions early in the new year of 1665. Before that could happen, however, Willoughby held a Christmas party at his Parham Hill estate. Allin gatecrashed, and a couple of days later was called into a private interview with Willoughby, in which the latter told Allin that until his case had been tried, they could not meet socially.

For reasons that might have been real or imagined, by this stage Allin was convinced that Willoughby was trying to get hold of his plantation, which was situated close to his own. (In fact, as proprietor, Willoughby could do pretty much what he liked.) Allin was now determined, Byam writes, to act like one of the 'noble Romans' he had been reading about. One night in the first week of January, Willoughby, Byam and the council were attending a small service in the upper dining room of Parham Hill. The chaplain was reading the lesson which, according to Byam, happened to be from II Samuel 3, which tells the story, against the backdrop of a civil war between Saul and David, of a defector, Abner son of Saul, who is trying to unify the divided nation. But David's lieutenant Joab assassinates Abner, mistakenly thinking he is a spy and traitor to his king's cause.

While this story was being told, Allin slipped unnoticed into the room, thanks to his disguise of a 'negro coat', presumably the garish livery in which the smartest planters now dressed their house slaves.

Allin approached Willoughby with his left hand extended, as if in greeting, but his right hidden behind his thigh. Suddenly, 'with a ghastly and direful countenance', he produced in his right hand a short but very sharp cutlass, and 'smote at his Excellencies head with all his fury'. The first blow hit Willoughby's skull – apparently so 'that his brains were seen to beat'. Willoughby raised his left hand in self-defence, causing a second blow to sever his fore- and middle fingers. He would have lost a third, had not the blade hit a large ring.

Byam was the first to grab the attacker, at which point Allin immediately stabbed himself in his right side and collapsed to the floor. Several of those present, crying 'Kill the dog!', wished to dispatch Allin on the spot, but instead his weapon was seized, and Byam 'secured him with a guard'.

Checking on Willoughby, Byam was relieved to find that his head wound was, after all, 'a glancing blow'. Allin, for his part, was treated by a surgeon, and then locked up for the night in Parham Hill. His self-inflicted wound remained 'a large orifice' and, in terrible pain, Allin cursed that he had been unable to kill himself. A chaplain was sent to see the prisoner. Allin told him he regretted only that he had failed to kill Willoughby, and as far as religion was concerned, to 'talk to the rabble, and not to him'. Later in the night, Allin tried to kill himself with a pistol that he had hidden about his person, but he could not get it to fire. He called the guard to give him a light for his pipe and clapped the burning coal to the gun's pan, 'but all would not discharge the pistol', and it was taken from him.

The next day Allin was loaded into a boat to be shipped to the prison at Torarica. During the journey he was 'seized with internal tortures, and in a short time became senseless and expired.' His 'carcass was delivered to the common Gaol', where Byam ordered 'several surgeons' to cut him open, upon which was discovered 'a Pill of Landocum undigested, some digested, and some that had passed into his Intestines'. The pills had apparently been obtained by bribing the doctor with a diamond ring. A letter was found from Allin to Willoughby: 'I have too much of the Roman in me to possess my own life, when I cannot enjoy it with freedom and honour,' Allin had written.

The crime of suicide 'meriting an unusual punishment', his naked carcass was dragged through the streets to the town's pillory, 'where a barbecue was erected'. There, as Byam gleefully relates, 'his Members were cut off, and flung in his face, they and his Bowels burnt under the Barbicue'. On the fire, too, went a 'seditious paper which he had left to be published after his death.' His head was cut off, and his body quartered, 'and when dry-barbicued or dry-roasted, after the Indian manner, his head was stuck on a pole at Parham, and his quarters put up at the most eminent places of the Colony.'

Willoughby slowly convalesced, and eventually left Suriname for Barbados on 9 May 1665, having missed important events elsewhere. It seems his visit had solved nothing.

Negotiations must have taken place about the terms of government and of land ownership under his new proprietorship. But on this occasion Willoughby seems to have left his charm and tact behind, appointing William Byam as lieutenant general of the colony and his deputy governor until further notice (the 'ambition of Perpetual Dominion' which Sanford had accused him of desiring thus achieved), and displaying nothing but self-interest when it came to the legal status of the planters' landholding. Allin's fellow planters were furious that they were now tenants, rather than freeholders. On Willoughby's departure,

Byam admits, the party feuds broke out again and 'strange jealousies' and 'great discontents' possessed the planters. Some 200 left the colony, and others threatened 'to desert the colony to some place where they might not be tenants at will.' Clearly Allin's protest, though extreme, was indicative of widespread disillusion.

Perhaps worst of all, Willoughby seems to have brought with him in his party some sort of infection, 'a most strange violent Feavor, burning within & yet ye same time, ye Feet & hands exceeding cold.' Just before his departure, an outbreak hit Torarica, and then spread to the neighbouring plantations, 'and swept many away'.

As it turned out, Willoughby's long-awaited visit was the first part of a disastrous process of the outside world inflicting itself on the new English colony. In Europe, tension was still building between the English and the Dutch. In fact, an unofficial war was already under way and set to spread.

Fourteen

WAR AND RUIN

'Holland, that scarce deserves the name of Land
As but th'Off-scouring of the British Sand . . .
This ingested vomit of the sea
Fell to the Dutch by just propriety.'

ANDREW MARVELL, 'THE CHARACTER
OF HOLLAND', 1653

In many respects the Dutch and the English should have been natural allies. Both nations were Protestant, outward-looking and commercially minded. During the previous century they had fought together against the power of Spain, and England had sent troops and money to help the Dutch in their struggle for independence. Now the strength and dazzling wealth of Louis XIV of France threatened them both.

However, it was their similarity that provoked conflict. The English and Dutch economies were competitive rather than complementary and from the 1600s, they became ever fiercer commercial rivals in Europe, Asia, Africa and America.

Competition in the Spice Islands of Indonesia, up for grabs as local Portuguese power waned, had led in 1623 to the Amboina 'massacre', when twenty English traders had been tortured by the Dutch (with what we would now call waterboarding) and executed, an outrage well publicised at the time and remembered whenever anti-Dutch sentiment required whipping up. When the Interregnum Parliament had tried to establish a monopoly for English ships in trade with the home country and colonies, a measure aimed directly at the Dutch, the two countries had fought a naval war in 1652–4. The English came out marginally on top, taking many more lucrative prizes, but nothing had been resolved.

At the Restoration, the returning English King was personally presented with 'The Dutch Gift' – a lavish collection of twenty-four paintings, including two by Titian, twelve sculptures and a yacht. The naive hope that this would prevent Charles reaffirming the earlier monopolistic Navigation Act failed amid growing English jealousy of the commercial supremacy of the United Provinces, whose merchant fleet was greater than all other European powers put together, making them the 'recognised carriers of Europe'. Over the past decades, England had lost trade in regions from the Baltic to the Mediterranean, from Asia to America. Moreover the Dutch were now preeminent in candle and soap production, dyewood processing, paper manufacturing, tobacco blending, sugar refining and many other industries.

This was the zenith of the Dutch 'Golden Age'. It was as if, John Evelyn noted, 'the Hollanders have taken a resolution to have the monarchy of trade of the whole world.' England wanted its share and, with four times the population of the United Provinces, was prepared to go to war to get it. As Pepys noted in his diary in February 1664, 'the trade of the world is too little for us two, therefore one must down.'

Driving this new aggression was a group of courtiers gathered around James, Duke of York, many of whom were investors in the new Royal Adventurers Company. And it would be the growing importance of the Africa Trade, particularly in slaves, that would provide the greatest impetus towards war.

At the end of 1663, the company sent the former Royalist privateer Sir Robert Holmes to West Africa to protect their interests. He interpreted this as licence to launch aggressive raids on Dutch trading posts. Johan de Witt, effective leader of the United Provinces, heard news of the English fleet and got a message to his admiral Michiel de Ruyter, then in the Mediterranean, to follow Holmes to Africa. There de Ruyter recaptured all the lost trading posts, as well as scooping up a huge quantity of booty. He then crossed the Atlantic determined to strike at the heart of English power in the Americas – Barbados.

The admiral's force arrived at the island on 20 April and engaged the forts guarding Bridgetown harbour. The governor, Francis Willoughby, was still recuperating in Suriname, but his nephew Henry Willoughby led a spirited defence, and the Dutch were driven off. De Ruyter returned to Europe, but not before capturing nearly twenty English vessels in the Leeward Islands.

In June, an English force under Richard Nicholls was sent against the Dutch North American settlement of New Netherland, comprising what are now the states of New York, Delaware and New Jersey. Three hundred soldiers from four warships went ashore on Long Island in August and moved west to Breuckelen (later Brooklyn), enlisting support from the English towns on Long Island and distributing handbills ahead of the advancing troops, offering fair treatment and generous terms to those who surrendered. The Dutch governor Peter Stuyvesant favoured resistance but the town's merchants were unconvinced. Stuyvesant surrendered the colony on 8 September.

The seizure was primarily motivated by a desire to close the loophole that had allowed English merchants to export their tobacco through the Dutch port and thereby avoid the terms of the Navigation Act. Neither side considered the capture itself particularly important, especially when compared to the gains to be made in the West African slave trade.

In retaliation for the de Ruyter raids, the English squadron in the Mediterranean was ordered to attack the

Dutch 'Smyrna convoy' from the Levant. There was an inconclusive battle off Cadiz in December 1664, which provoked the States-General of the United Provinces to declare war on 14 January 1665.

With the departure of de Ruyter's fleet from the theatre, the English launched a broad offensive in the Caribbean. From Port Royal in Jamaica, Thomas Modyford, governor there since 1664, unleashed his unofficial force of buccaneers, described by Modyford as '1,500 lusty fellows'. In August, led by Colonel Sir Edward Morgan, uncle of the better-known Henry, they captured the well-defended Dutch islands of Saba and St Eustacius, carrying away 700 slaves and huge amounts of merchandise. (For Edward Morgan, it was his last adventure: as Modyford reported to London, 'the good old Colonel leaping out of the boat, and being a corpulent man got a strain, and his spirit being great he pursued over earnestly the enemy on a hot day, so that he surfeited and suddenly died.') Nonetheless, the buccaneers then prepared to attack Curaçao and Tobago. 'When the Dutch have lost one or two small islands more, they will not have a foot of ground in all America,' the English triumphantly reported back to London.

In contrast to the crowded West Indian islands, the Europeans who had settled on the 1,200-mile Wild Coast between the Amazon and the Orinoco had until this time been living in peace with each other. The menace of Spanish power, the threat of the indigenous people and the vast area available for development had led to an almost unbroken tradition of local friendship and cooperation between the English, Dutch and French.

By mid-1665, there were four distinct Dutch settlements, two French and one English. Furthest to the south-east, near where Leigh and Harcourt's English settlements had failed, was the small Dutch colony of Aprowaco. Although some fruit trees had been planted, it was essentially a trading station, guarded by a block house and palisades. Next along the coast was Cayenne, occupied once again by the French since 1664. Here, Fort St Louis protected a small cluster of dwellings, and there was a little town known as Armyra on the other side of the island. The occupants were mainly involved with the annatto dye trade, although there was some sugar production. A smaller settlement further west on the River Sinnamari constituted the second French colony.

Willoughbyland was next, then three fairly closely bunched Dutch settlements at Berbice, Essequibo and Pomeroon, the last being the oldest and most developed, with a number of thriving sugar plantations.

According to William Byam, May 1665 saw the colony of Willoughbyland 'in its meridian and after this month had its declination and went ever retrograde'. In May there was a considerable force of some 1,000 men able to bear

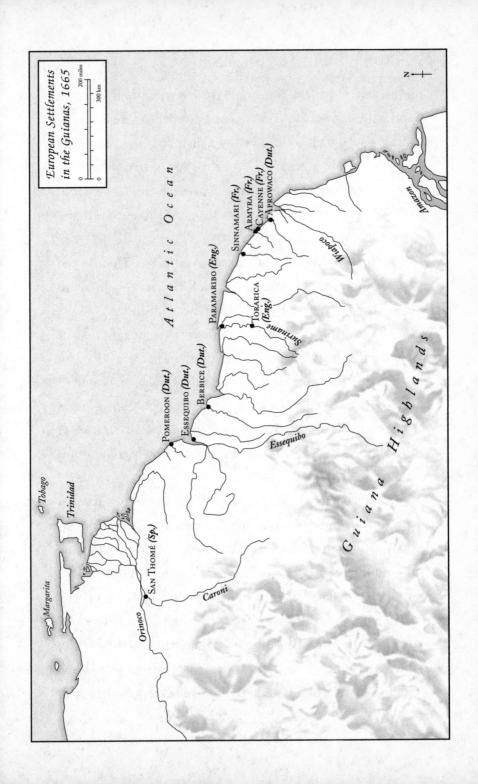

European Settlements
in the Guianas, 1665

arms, even if there were only weapons for half of them and a shortage of ammunition and powder. As the narrator of *Oroonoko* had noticed, 'the English had none but rusty swords . . . the guns also . . . for 'tis in the nature of that country to rust and eat up iron.' There were, however, as per Willoughby's instructions, six guns mounted on the riverbank at Paramaribo.

For most of 1665, Guiana remained at peace. Then, at the end of the year, came the order from King Charles himself to 'root the Dutch out of all places in the West Indies'.

Thus in December, Willoughby sent a regiment of about 300 men from Barbados to attack the Dutch in Tobago. When they arrived, they found that they had been beaten to the prize by two days by a force of English buccaneers from Jamaica under the command of Henry Morgan. So instead they turned their attack on the nearby Dutch colonies on the mainland.

The regiment was led by Major John Scott. As was often the case in the history of the empire, it was the man on the spot, often of an unconventional nature, who made the running. Scott, who has been described as 'one of the most picturesque and far-wandering scoundrels of his time', and 'born to work mischief', is a complicated figure to understand, partly because he is himself the author of the fullest account we have of his exploits. He appears to have originated in Ashford, Kent, then travelled to Massachusetts as an indentured labourer in about 1643 with his destitute mother, 'a poor bankrupt miller's wife'. However, when he explained to people who he was and where he came from, no two explanations quite agreed with each other. In North America, he traded with the indigenous people, while possibly working as a blacksmith. At one point in 1654 he was imprisoned by the Dutch in New Amsterdam after nocturnal raids on their property were blamed on him. It seems that in 1660 he was briefly back in England, then on the move again, pursued by the widow of a man he reportedly swindled out of £2,000.

The Restoration, with its uncertainty and upheaval, offered an unparalleled opportunity for not over-scrupulous men like Scott to advance their fortunes. Calling himself a colonel, in January 1664 Scott led an unauthorised attack on the Dutch settlement of Breuckelen. For this offence, or possibly for selling land in Long Island that he did not own, he was arrested and imprisoned by the English authorities. He escaped from gaol and fled to Barbados, where, no doubt deploying his notorious 'smooth tongue', he somehow persuaded Willoughby to give him a commission in the island's militia.

Pre-empted at Tobago, he took his frustration out on the Dutch settlements of Essequibo and Pomeroon. Their small forts were ruthlessly stormed amid much bloodshed, and then, as he wrote, he 'burnt and destroyed the enemy's towns, goods, and settlements to the value of 160,000l'. Moving on to Berbice, he found it already under attack by English privateers, so he returned to Barbados with his loot, leaving small garrisons at Pomeroon – fifty men under Captain Bawlston – and Essequibo – twenty-eight men under Captain Keene. According to Scott, he urged Willoughby to strengthen or amalgamate these garrisons, but nothing was done.

About three months later, on orders from Willoughby, Byam sent a Captain Peter Wroth from Suriname with a small party to attack the Dutch colony to the south-east at Aprowaco. According to Byam's own account, this 'was effectually done, their Armes, Slaves, Copper &c brought hither, that small Colony destroyed.' Thus by the end of March 1666, all the Dutch mainland settlements, with the exception of Berbice, where the privateer attack had been repelled, had, indeed, been 'rooted out'.

The following month, Byam received a request from the commander of Cayenne, Monsieur de Lézy, who 'advised me of the certainty of the eruption of war between our two crowns' and 'earnestly solicited, that notwithstanding the war abroad, yet that we might continue friends.'

Byam, aware that thanks to the depredations of the fever still raging through the colony it was 'not at that time in a Condition to offend, nor well to defend itself', replied to the French governor that he would have to attack if ordered, but

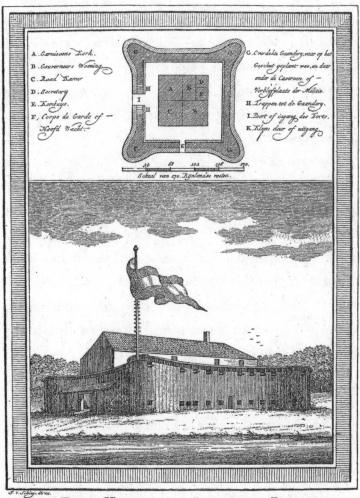

HET FORT NASSAU OP DE COLONIE DE BERBICE.

Fort Nassau, which would successfully guard the Dutch colony of Berbice from English attack.

would give notice of it. In the meantime, Byam appealed to Willoughby in Barbados for 'a large supply of arms and ammunition'. But no ship came, and 'finding our condition very sad and exposed', he summoned the council and assembly to pass an act ordering every tenth 'working Negro' to be sent to Paramaribo to labour on preparing materials for the fort. The town's garrison was strengthened, and lookouts posted at the river mouth.

Soon afterwards, the news reached Byam that in January France had indeed joined the Dutch in their war against England, and in June 1666, on a 'vessel from Barbados', he heard that in April the French had taken the English half of St Kitts amid great bloodshed and destruction. With this news came orders from Willoughby that the French colonies in Guiana should be attacked in revenge. In the assembly at Torarica there were worries that dispatching able-bodied men for this mission would fatally weaken the English colony, particularly as there were rumours of a joint Dutch and Arawak force readying itself to take revenge for Major Scott's depredations at Pomeroon and Essequibo. In the event, seventy men under Captain William Cowell were sent against Sinnamari, the smaller French colony. Eighty under Captain Christopher Rendar set out in canoes to the north-west to relieve the English garrisons left by Major Scott holding Pomeroon and Essequibo.

Cowell's men arrived at Sinnamari on 14 August and sent

in a letter denouncing the armistice. Before dawn the next morning, they successfully stormed the fort, killing seven of the French defenders and taking prisoner the governor and fifty men before 'utterly destroying the whole Colony'. So, for a brief moment, as Scott writes, 'the English could boast of the possession of all that part of Guiana' from Cayenne to the Orinoco, with the exception of Berbice.

The other expedition, however, was less successful. Rendar's men attacked a couple of villages of 'Arawaks' allied to the Dutch, killing thirty and capturing seventy, but they were too late to save the tiny English garrisons at Essequibo and Pomeroon. In the former, the twenty-eight men under Captain Keene, cut off and starving, had surrendered about two weeks before to a Dutch force from Berbice, under Commander Bergenaar, which had advanced along a ten-mile path through the jungle that linked the two settlements.

At Pomeroon, where the fifty-man garrison led by Captain Bawlston had come under attack from a far superior joint French and Dutch force, it was even worse. Here, despite promises of safe passage, the French 'most inhumanely delivered [the English captives] to the Arawaks at the mouth of the river to be massacred.' The peaceful coexistence of the Europeans that had preceded the arrival of Major Scott was now a distant memory.

Fifteen

ASTREA AND CELADON

'Consider, then, my beautiful Astrea,
that I have suffered long enough, and that
it is now time that you permit me
to play the role of Céladon.'

HONORÉ D'URFÉ, *L'ASTRÉE*

Back in Willoughbyland, whilst battles were played out elsewhere, the fever that had been brought with Willoughby's party and broken out in May the previous year had continued 'violently'; by August it had killed 200 men 'and very many women and children'. Amongst those to die were Aphra Behn's friend George Marten and the Nonconformist pamphleteer Henry Adis. Particularly badly hit, according to Byam, were the 'few masons, and many negroes which were at work on the fort'. Together with the difficulty of cutting the shellstone with axes, this 'very much retarded the work'.

In the same month a ship arrived from Barbados with six barrels of powder and some 'match'. This was 'exceeding welcome', though Byam sent the ship back to plead for ammunition and more powder and to 'present to his excellency the sad and dangerous condition of our colony'. There was a little ammunition but no powder to spare in Barbados, and the returning ship also brought the shocking news that Francis Lord Willoughby, Byam's protector and the 'essence' of Willoughbyland, was dead.

As early as December the previous year, Willoughby had been directly warned by the King that conflict with France was coming, and that their first blow would fall in St Kitts, which had been uneasily divided between the French and English since its first colonisation. To give him his due, Willoughby had prepared well, so that when the attack came in April 1666, the English forces, bolstered by buccaneers from Jamaica, had far outnumbered their French enemies. Yet the island was still lost, thanks to incompetence and in-fighting on the part of the English. For Willoughby, it was a personal blow to his standing with the King. It hadn't helped that Willoughby was at the same time seeking permission to return to England to answer complaints of arbitrary government made against him by Barbadian speaker of the assembly and friend of the Sanfords, Samuel Farmer. Farmer had tried to present Willoughby with what he called 'a petition of right', and had found himself arrested and banished.

So when in July two frigates had arrived at Barbados from England, at last giving him some naval muscle,

Willoughby rushed to retake St Kitts. He had already shipped 1,500 men to nearby Antigua, commanded by his nephew, Henry. Now he commandeered eight large vessels on to which he poured 1,000 more locally raised men, as well as arms for the Antiguan force. With Willoughby himself on board the flagship, the fleet set sail on 18 July. It was a perilous time to take to the sea, as Willoughby ought to have known: the hurricane season was almost upon them.

The fleet was anchored off Guadeloupe eight days later when without warning a 'violent storm' fell upon it. The entire armada was wrecked or dispersed, and what naval power England had been able to muster in the theatre was sunk. Of Lord Willoughby and his warship there was no trace, except the couch from his cabin and some 'peeces of a ship' washed up at Montserrat.

At a stroke, the English had lost control of the seas to their enemies. In November a force of seven French warships under Admiral Joseph-Antoine de La Barre descended on Antigua, which was then ransacked. Everything was plundered, from slaves to sugar equipment to provisions. Once the French departed, those English who had not fled were left defenceless against the revenges of the indigenous people from nearby islands with whom they had been fighting a long battle. Montserrat followed suit soon afterwards with similar destruction. Later that month in Willoughbyland Byam heard that the seven

French warships were now at Cayenne. In December he received 'ye dismall news of ye Burning of London' and a warning that 'we might daily expect a French fleet from Leeward, who were victorious there to attack us.'

Byam ordered the Willougbyland settlers to build shelters and store up provisions 'over swamps and in remote parts'. He set lookouts in canoes at the river mouth, directed the blocking of the Para and Serino creeks with large felled trees and appointed officers for a general levy. Every man who could bear arms was to be ready for what seemed like an inevitable attack.

In home waters there had been a significant victory for the English fleet over the Dutch at the battle of Lowestoft in June 1665, but attritional battles at sea the following summer had left the Royal Navy dangerously weak. At the beginning of the conflict Parliament had voted the King a very large sum – £2.5 million – as a war chest but it had been spent quickly and badly, while the Dutch spent twice as much: for every English warship turned out, they built seven. Furthermore, large parts of England were badly hit by the plague, seen by many as punishment for Charles's licentious court. In the summer and autumn of 1665, thousands were dying in London every week. Only in February 1666 was it thought safe enough for the court to return to Whitehall from its exile in Oxford.

*The culmination of the Anglo-Dutch struggle for control of home waters
was a massive naval battle off the Kent coast over the first four days of June
1666. But commercial rivalry and naval conflict spread across the globe.*

Charles's government, having made so many domestic
enemies through its persecution of Nonconformists,
remained insecure, unsure of either popular support or its
future. Many English religious or political dissidents had
ended up in the United Provinces, whose leader Johan de
Witt was ardently republican. There was even an English
regiment in Dutch pay. It was this potential union of a
foreign belligerent with domestic enemies that most alarmed
King Charles, who of course had been restored thanks to
English domestic plotting rather than by force of arms

(as would be the case in 1688, when the main Stuart dynasty ended). The English authorities urgently needed agents to infiltrate these dissident groups, as well as to provide the best possible information on Dutch military plans.

When William Scot had arrived in Rotterdam from Willoughbyland, he had made contact with anti-Royalist English there and in The Hague. He had a sister in Rotterdam, married to an Englishman, Richard Sykes. William Sykes, Richard's brother, was a merchant and spy for the Dutch, liaising with English dissidents in the Low Countries.

After the English naval victory at Lowestoft in June 1665, perhaps thinking the war was about to be won, Scot had made contact through an intermediary with the English government, offering information about a plot for simultaneous anti-Royalist uprisings in Yorkshire and the West Country, aided by the Dutch. Scot hoped in return for 'a large sum for his secret'. However, Scot slightly over-egged the pudding by falsely including in the list of conspirators all the biggest English republican fish still at large.

When this effort failed, he got in touch with two English Royalist agents in Holland, Nicholas Oudart and Thomas Corney, offering to 'come over', but then promptly betrayed them to the Dutch. In return, he was given a position in the English regiment in Dutch pay in Holland. An anonymous letter received by the London government in August 1665 reports that William Scot was now on a retainer of 1,000 rixdollars a year from Dutch leader de Witt.

In March the following year Scot found himself on a well-publicised list, along with thirteen others of the English regiment wanted for treason. In fact, he wasn't just on the list, he was the first name, and the only one with a rather chilling addition: 'son of Thos. Scot, executed for high treason'.

Scot was clearly rattled. Soon afterwards he contacted the secretary of state, Lord Arlington, pleading for a pardon and money for turning double agent. So now the English authorities needed someone to meet him to assess whether he was useful or trustworthy.

Soon after her return to London in the spring of 1664, Aphra Johnson became Mrs Behn. Of Mr Behn little is known, except that he was of Dutch or north German extraction. He might have been a merchant sailor, and could even have been working on the ship that brought Aphra back from Suriname. Sometime before the summer of 1666, Mr Behn seems to have died, possibly from the plague. He does not appear to have left much of an inheritance, because Aphra would henceforth have to support herself.

Behn had presented the exotic feathers, given to her on her trip upriver in Suriname, to Thomas Killigrew for whom she may have worked before the Restoration. Killigrew still dabbled in intelligence, though thanks to his closeness to the King he had been appointed, without any particular expertise, to chief of the King's Company of actors, one of only two patent theatre companies. The feathers would feature in a production of Dryden and Robert Howard's *The Indian Queen*, and in the sequel *The Indian Emperor*; the 'speckled plumes' were much admired.

If Aphra was hoping that Killigrew might put on her play *The Young King*, she would be disappointed. In June 1665, all the London theatres were closed down as the plague worsened in the city.

In the autumn of 1666, however, Killigrew approached her about another matter. Lord Arlington and he had probably seen Byam's letter to Harley mentioning Behn and Scot's 'sympathetical passion' (Harley was back in England and also involved with intelligence). Scot was known to be 'lewd', so who better to send than attractive Aphra Behn to charm him into giving them the information they wanted, and perhaps dropping his guard along the way? Alternatively she may have been requested by William Scot himself.

So, as Behn later wrote, she undertook a mission 'Unusual with my Sex, or to my Years'. It was certainly highly dangerous: she could be arrested in Holland or set upon anywhere by anti-Royalists; furthermore, Scot had shown his capacity for betrayal, and despite their history might easily give up Aphra to appease his Dutch paymasters or fellow dissident 'brethren'.

At the beginning of August 1666, Behn, together with the familiar entourage of her brother, mother and maid, left Gravesend aboard the *Castel Rodrigo* bound for Ostend in the Spanish Netherlands. Once again, her code names were 'Astrea' and 'Agent 160'. Ostend was badly hit by the plague, so the vessel unloaded at Passchendaele. From there she proceeded to Bruges, then Antwerp, very near the border with the United Provinces. On 15 August, Behn and Scot – code-named Astrea and Celadon on this occasion – met for the first time since Suriname. Scot was a nervous wreck, fearing lest his Dutch employers hear of the meeting, or of being snatched by agents from England and bundled in chains across the Channel, as had happened to fugitive regicides three years earlier. Furthermore, Corney, unexpectedly released in January 1666, was in Flanders and had vowed to kill Scot for betraying him to the Dutch.

Behn was staying at a small guest house, the Rosa Noble, but Scot insisted that she hire a coach so they could talk while keeping on the move and check if they were being followed. He also declined to produce anything incriminating in his own hand: Behn had to write it all down for him.

She had been equipped with a shopping list of information which Scot was to provide in return for his pardon and some sort of payment: what the English dissidents or 'fanatics' were up to; who was spying for the Dutch in England; what plans existed for the French and Dutch fleets to combine forces; recent losses at sea; the expected date of arrival of the valuable East India convoy.

After the meeting, Aphra Behn reported back to her handler in London, Major James Halsall. Scot had been 'at first shy', she wrote, using the agreed codes, but she had warmed him up, and 'he became by arguments extremely willing to undertake the service.'

Scot wanted Behn to go to Holland for their next meeting, as Dutch suspicions would likely be raised by him crossing the border. But Behn was warned by the English in Antwerp that this was too dangerous. Scot would have to come to her, the cost of which would be borne by her along with the expense of private messengers carrying their communications. She had been issued with £50, but it was running out fast.

They met again at the end of August at a little house a few miles outside Antwerp. 'Celadon leaves nothing unsaid to beget confidence, seems earnest in his wish to serve,' Behn reported to Halsall. But the Dutch had stopped paying the English regiment properly and Scot was so short of money that he could not leave Amsterdam without difficulty because of his debts there. Scot gave Aphra a titbit of information about a Dutch spy arrested in England, but insisted that 'he must be assured of his pardon' before he could 'do service'. Scot wanted to return home to England, but was never going to make the mistake of his father and do so without a written pardon clutched in his hand.

The next letter from Behn was to Thomas Killigrew; Halsall had failed to reply to her last message. Scot was now telling 'everything on her bare word', but he had to have money. So too now did Behn, reporting that she owed £50, thanks to the cost of getting Scot to Antwerp, her expensive lodging and the outlay on personal messengers between the two of them. She wrote to Killigrew again five days later saying she had 'pawned her very rings to get the man' and now she needed £100.

Scot was then promised his pardon by Halsall. Aphra's brother was standing by to go and pick it up; but it was never produced. Neither was the promised money. Although the chaos caused by the Great Fire of London at the beginning of September might have been a contributory factor, it seems that Arlington and Killigrew were happy to wring out of Scot whatever information he had and then discard him, perhaps because he hadn't proven his worth, or because he simply wasn't to be trusted given his father's regicide status and his own misdemeanours.

Clearly Aphra believed the offer she was instructed to make to Scot was genuine. Whether he was sincere in his wish to 'serve the King as his lawful sovereign' as he claimed is less easy to determine. There was one bit of information he offered that should have been taken more seriously: Scot reported of a Dutch plan involving sinking ships in the mouth of the Thames as part of an attack upriver. In the light of what happened the following year, perhaps this should have been acted on. Apart from that, there was little that Scot gave them that Arlington did not already know, or could have picked up from the printed news-sheets.

Aphra, for her part, rather than coolly assessing Scot's value and trustworthiness, became his advocate, declaring that she 'believed in him all things'. United in mutual financial desperation, Aphra and William seem to have re-established their old intimacy. When at last it became clear that Scot – now referred to as 'my friend' and 'the poore man' – was not going to be pardoned or paid, Behn wrote of her regret that she had been put in the position of having to 'fool him so long' with vain expectations.

For his part, William Scot had had enough. Before the end of the year he returned to service for the Dutch (if he had ever left it), bringing with him what turned out to be very useful information indeed.

He might have got the idea from one of the questions Aphra Behn brought with her for him to answer: whether the Dutch had 'any design of attempting anything by land in any of the King's dominions'. The English had ignored, and failed to pay for, his advice about possible landings in England, so now he advised the Dutch, in particular the authorities in Zeeland in whose jurisdiction he had lived in Rotterdam, to attack the English colony of Willoughbyland.

Not only did Scot have information from his own recent trip there, he was also most likely still in touch with his brother Richard and other of the Roundhead 'brethren' in the colony. Therefore he would have been able to pass on intelligence about defences (or lack of them), about the disease that had crippled the English militia, and about the large body of anti-Royalist settlers likely to defect at the first opportunity.

The Dutch, learning of these weaknesses and still smarting from the depredations of Major John Scot on their lucrative and peaceful settlements in Guiana, recognised that a comparatively small force might win them a great victory.

Sixteen

THE FALL OF FORT WILLOUGHBY

'In February arrived a Dutch fleet from
Zealand, by the advice of Scot, to take the
colony, which found us in a most weak
condition, near half our men dead and half
that were living, miserably weak, ill armed.'

BYAM TO SIR ROBERT HARLEY, FROM ANTIGUA,
6 NOVEMBER 1668

The motion to launch the expedition to Willoughbyland
was tabled by Zeeland Grand Pensionary Justus de
Huybert, and approved by the States' council. By the end of
December 1666 the force was assembled: three frigates, each
with twenty-eight to thirty-six guns, a smaller 'Jacht' with
fourteen guns, a two-master dogger boat with six guns, and
two other small shallow-drafted vessels. In addition to the
regular crew of about 750 sailors, 225 soldiers were on the
ships, led by Julius Lichtenbergh and Maurice de Rame. In

overall command was Admiral Abraham Crijnssen, who had distinguished himself during the battle of the Downs, the decisive naval defeat of Spain by the Dutch in 1639.

It was a comparatively modest force, indicating that the Zeelanders had good intelligence on the weakness of Willoughbyland. The orders for Crijnssen were to 'take the English by surprise' and to 'seek fortune'. It was imperative that any English ship encountered on the way be seized, so that no warning would precede their descent on Suriname. There was to be as little bloodshed as possible, and prisoners of war were to be well treated.

Later described by a nineteenth-century Dutch historian as 'courageous sealions', the fleet set sail on 30 December. Without mishap, and successfully scooping up the ships – one Irish and one from New England – which they encountered on their way, they reached Cayenne in late February. The governor there, de Lézy, urged them to wait for the arrival of Admiral de La Barre's ships, still away to the north – the French rather fancied conquering Willoughbyland themselves – but Crijnssen pressed on along the coast.

On Friday 25 February the men stationed as lookouts at the mouth of the Suriname river saw seven ships approaching quickly from the east. A canoe was straight away dispatched upriver to take the news to Byam at Fort Willoughby, while the English tried to establish the identity of the vessels. At first they assumed they were the French ships rumoured to have been at Cayenne in November. There was considerable relief when the ships raised English flags, but the Dutch were unable to answer signals from the English correctly and so were at last identified as foes.

On hearing the news, Byam 'sent orders into the country' – presumably an appeal for urgent reinforcements from Torarica and the surrounding plantations – and directed that all buildings within musket shot of the fort be pulled down or burnt, and gloomily surveyed his position.

Fort Willoughby was, for reasons of ground conditions, poorly sited behind an outcrop that cut off the view downriver. Nevertheless it was still the key to the colony. Its loss would trap the English upriver, leaving them unable to trade or even subsist for long.

Work on the vital defences of the fort had been proceeding desperately slowly. By January gates had at last been set up, but the riverside walls, though thick, were barely six feet high in places and only one bastion of the planned pentagonal five had been completed. A month later another was half built and the riverside walls had risen to ten feet, with a palisade of sharpened tree trunks in front, but as Byam wrote afterwards, it was still only 'half a fort'.

The fort's armament was motley, to say the least. Byam had twenty-one guns, but of those, nine had no carriages and were thus unusable. The 'most serviceable gun' was a 'culverin', which fired a hefty eighteen-pound shot, but it had no ammunition of the right size. There was one demi-culverin, firing nine-pound shot, but the rest of the guns were small four- or five-pounders. For all of these there were only half a dozen cases of gunpowder. At the same time, provisions were in short supply.

To defend the half-built fort, Byam had only a hundred men. Sixty enslaved Africans who had been working on the walls now found a lance thrust into their hands with orders to stand by, ready to counter-attack if the fort was breached.

Byam wrote his account of these events, which later became the official English version, to defend himself against charges of cowardice, for which he would face a court martial. He is therefore careful to stress the hopeless weakness of the situation he faced. According to his reckoning, the Willoughbyland militia of 1,000 men of May 1665 (albeit poorly armed) had shrunk to 700 by July and to 500 by the end of the year. To blame were the 'desertions' following Willoughby's fairly disastrous descent on his realm, and also the contagion his party had left behind. Now a full-scale epidemic, the fever had carried off 500 by the beginning of 1667, including 40 of the colony's senior planters and officers, 'a great part of the chiefest men of the land'. Of the 500 militia remaining, Byam reports, 200 were too sick or lame to be able to fight. The epidemic had affected everyone. 'Not a family that I know escaped it,'

Byam writes. 'Miserable were ye Cryes, & dejected were ye Spirits of all.'

For many communities and nations, an outside threat serves to unite people. In Willoughbyland this spectacularly failed to happen. More than anything, it seems the colony was suffering a crisis of confidence, of leadership, of morale. The proprietor, Francis Willoughby, was dead. Whether settlers were of the faction that celebrated or despaired at the news, it had added to the uncertainty prevalent since the Restoration. Black slaves and white servants were alike becoming ever more rebellious. Byam himself had been ill – 'weak & exceeding lame' – since August the previous year, probably from gout. Now, he says, he could hardly walk.

Although the French were feared by the English, following their ransacking of St Kitts, Antigua and Montserrat, there was no particular antagonism towards the Dutch, with whom there were many personal and business ties as well as political sympathy among the colony's republican 'brethren'. One English militia captain stationed upcountry, hearing that it was the Dutch in the river rather than the French as had been rumoured, 'stript his colours and refused to fight, and some of the soldiers also'. Many of the colony's large Jewish population were actually Dutch-born. They had come to Willoughbyland, in the main via Brazil and Cayenne, attracted by the chance to 'establish a community free from aristocratic tendencies'. The proprietorship of

Willoughby had sat awkwardly with this ambition and a switch to Dutch control looked appealing.

Yet there was a deeper malaise at work that made the enemy almost irrelevant. As the Sanford and Allin affairs had shown, the planters were deeply, even murderously, divided amongst themselves. Disease had, indeed, made every home a place of grief and loss. As the best estates had been sold to absentee owners such as the greedy and corrupt Sir Robert Harley, and the cruelties and tyrannies of slavery had defined a new, ugly way of life, so the 'brave land' of the 1650s now seemed an age ago. The nationalist, heroic purpose of it all had leeched away. The Willoughbyland they would have fought to defend was no more.

On Saturday 26 February, Crijnssen moved his fleet to within a mile of the fort and anchored by the opposite bank. A drummer boy was sent in a small vessel towards the fort, but he was intercepted midstream where he handed over a letter in French and Dutch addressed to William Byam. In it, Crijnssen offered the Willoughbylanders security in their possessions if they surrendered. Otherwise, he wrote, 'I am resolved to attack you by Sea & Land, with the design of killing all that shall oppose, not giving Quarter to any one.' He demanded an answer within a quarter of an hour. Byam responded that he had been commanded to defend the fort, which he would try to do 'against all opposers; and so you might act your hostility as soon as you please.'

At about seven o'clock the next morning, at high tide, the three frigates and the smaller gunboat sailed up as close to the fort as they could and opened fire. This continued, Byam writes, 'with all the nimble fury they could for three hours.' The English gunners returned fire, but if they caused any damage to the Dutch ships, no one thought it worth recording. For the fort's defenders, though, it was a different story. Two of the English guns were quickly 'dismounted'. Because of the height of the river after the rainy season, and the lowness of the fort's walls, 'the enemy commanded from their decks and quarter deck above half of the inside of the fort, scouring two of the curtains, where our men were to stand to oppose.' Even

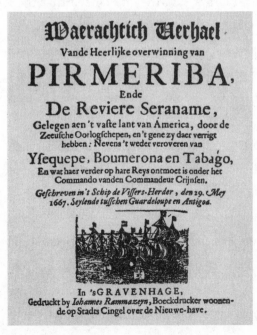

'The True Story Of the Glorious conquest of PIRMERIBA, and The River Seraname ...' A contemporary Dutch account that casts serious doubts on Byam's version of events around the loss of Fort Willoughby.

the completed bastion 'where we thought our men secure' took direct hits: 'they shivered 2 of our men's legs and thighs'. Meanwhile, writes Byam, 'Our Negroes whom I had armed with lances to oppose an assault, lay flat on their bellies.'

Owing to the lowness of the walls, the attackers were able to shoot over the riverside defences and take those opposite in reverse. Seeing this, Crijnssen piled as many men as he could – some 700 equipped with scaling ladders and grenades – into his remaining three vessels and put them down a short distance from the fort to attack from the landward side.

At this point, Byam's resistance crumbled. He called together his officers, he says, and they all agreed that their position was untenable as the walls on that side could not be manned. Even before the Dutch troops had formed up to attack, a white flag was raised by the English.

Byam asked for terms, agreeing to surrender the fort on the condition that the governor and his soldiers could march forth with their arms and flying colours, and be at liberty to go where they pleased, taking with them all they had except artillery, ammunition and provisions (of which they had precious little remaining, anyway).

After the surrender, the Dutch reneged, demanding weapons from the soldiers and taking the sixty black slaves who were in the fort. To deepen Byam's misery, of the ninety or so men he had, when promised by Crijnssen they could keep their property if they turned coat, 'most immediately clave to the Dutch' and 'promised to show them every creek and corner of the country, and direct them where our provisions, cattle and negroes were hid.'

'A big blessed victory!' declares a Dutch account of the battle, written two months later from eye-witness reports. 'In so many ways God's strange blessing has been apparent': the weather had been kind; only one Dutch soldier had been killed; and because 'Willoughby . . . had for a long time now been tormenting the inhabitants by very strict government . . . they were now fed up with his strictness and longed to be rid of it.'

It was a great victory for Zeeland, he continues, because 'the most beautiful river of the entire coast has been conquered . . . with wonderful plantations where such beautiful sugar is being produced, similar to what Brazil used to render. If with God's will this can be kept, it may well be turned into another Brazil.'

Most fortunate of all for the attackers, 'a strange blessing', he continues, was that a 'few hours late' 600 reinforcements arrived, 'because if they had been on time, without a doubt the victory would have been more difficult and costly.'

Byam, in his account, keen to stress the inevitability of his surrender, fails to mention how this force nearly rescued the situation; in fact, as we've seen, he claimed to have only 300 fit men in the entire colony. There seems little reason for the Dutch source to invent these men, although of course their number might have been exaggerated. But their existence does make Byam's capitulation seem hasty. If he had held out a little longer, or if he had garrisoned the fort with some of these men, the outcome could have been very different.

According to his version of events, Byam left the fort that night and at about two o'clock in the morning, two leagues upriver, he encountered Captain Clerke with fourteen 'periagoes from above, coming down to my assistance, whom I informed of the necessity of the surrender'. The fourteen canoes would not have held 600 men, and this was now many more than 'a few hours' after the surrender. Thus in Byam's version, unlike the Dutch one, the arrival of reinforcements was much too little too late, and had no bearing on his decision to capitulate.

Byam's account of what occurred next is somewhat confused. When he reached Torarica he seems to have tried to raise a force to counter-attack, and by accepting 'Jews and all, old and young, sick and well' gathered 168 men, who were piled into the fourteen canoes, along with 'negroes, & some Indians that paddled the boats'. He also had 'many Indians with bundles of war-arrows', but they had no provisions 'so that hunger inforced them quickly to return'. It's not clear what then happened. No attack was made on the captured fort, so perhaps they were merely guarding the riverside plantations between Paramaribo and Torarica.

Byam also called together what remained of Willoughbyland's council and assembly, and discussed the best course of action – to fight on, or to accept the generous terms offered by the Dutch. A few did, perhaps for the record, rail against the enemies of the King and vow to continue fighting, even if it meant retreating to the jungle and launching a guerrilla war. But reason, combined with business interest – the wish to preserve their plantations, built up 'by many years industry, and the painful sweat of their brows' – prevailed rather quickly. The assembly then drafted a document outlining the reasons why to fight on was impossible: their leader, Byam, was 'by his infirmity and great distemper' unable to operate, and his second in command Sergeant Major Thomas Noell was 'very dangerously sick'; they were outnumbered, and out of powder and ammunition as well as provisions and medicine; there had been a wave of desertions and men refusing to fight. (The leader of the Jewish community, Joseph Nassy, had already accepted a position in the new Dutch administration, and the colony's Jews had been declared to count as if born Dutch.) 'Undoubtedly,' the assembly noted, 'Christian servants and persons dishonest and in debt' would speedily desert and the black slaves were already 'killing our stock, breaking open houses, threatening our women, and some flying into the woods in rebellion.'

Furthermore, the Dutch seemed the least bad option. The arrival of the French was 'hourly expected', 'of whose merciless cruelty the English in the Neighbour Islands have lately had very sad experience.' And from the west, 'we also feare the invasion of the Arawack Indians, who will effect such mischiefe as will consequently produce the ruining of us all.'

Thus two hostages – William Parker and Angus Story – were handed over to the Dutch and peace negotiations began. The terms of the treaty took time, as neither side spoke the other's language well. After two days, agreement was reached. Those English planters resident in the colony were to keep their estates; the Dutch had come for Suriname's sugar, of which they demanded an indemnity of 100,000 pounds in weight, and wanted the growing and processing to continue as smoothly as possible. However, all Willoughby's property was forfeit, as was that of any other absentee planter, including Harley's 'very thriving stock of cattle at St Johns'. These were taken to Parham Hill (also confiscated), where 'some they killed and disposed of others'. The English were required to swear an oath of loyalty to the Dutch republic but in terms that made it only applicable when resident in Suriname. Freedom of conscience was also offered, as well as equal treatment for planters of all nationalities.

At around midnight on 6 March, on board the Dutch flagship the *Zeelandia*, the twenty-one articles of the agreement were finally signed by Crijnssen and Byam, who then retreated to his own plantation. Crijnssen turned his attention to the fort, now renamed Fort Zeelandia. He demanded sixty slaves to work for four months on its improvement under the direction of Maurice de Rame, who was to be the acting governor of the colony. Fifteen pieces of artillery and 120 men were left to guard it, supplied with plenty of ammunition and provisions for six months.

Crijnssen loaded his ships with his booty – worth, apparently, as much as 400,000 florins (about £40,000) – and sailed north, recapturing Tobago in April and St. Eustatius at the beginning of May. He then met up with de La Barre's French force, with a view to invading Nevis, but their joint fleet was scattered in a confused clash with an English force under Commodore John Berry. Thereafter Crijnssen headed to Virginia, where he captured a valuable cargo of tobacco, before returning to Zeeland to a hero's welcome.

William Willoughby, younger brother of Francis, had inherited the governorship of the Caribbees and the proprietorship of Suriname after Francis's death and was now in Barbados. He was appalled at the loss of the colony into which so much of the family fortune had been sunk, writing to London that it was 'pitifully surrendered without resistance' to a load of 'brewers and cheesemongers'. For William's brother Francis, Byam had been a right-hand man. For William he was a coward and traitor. Prompted by Robert Sanford, Byam's old 'inveterate and malicious enemy', William Willoughby determined to try Byam for cowardice.

Byam, stressing the weakness of Willoughbyland due to factors beyond his control – the sickness, the lack of gunpowder – and no doubt employing what Aphra Behn called his ' fawning fair-tongue', would be acquitted at the subsequent court martial, to Willoughby's fury. By then, however, there had been further dramatic events in the colony.

Seventeen

VICTORY AND ANGUISH

'May all offences, injuries, damages and
losses . . . on either side sustained during
this war heretofore be buried in oblivion and
completely erased from memory, as if
no such things had ever occurred.'

TREATY OF BREDA, JULY 1667

Willoughby's chance for redress came in the middle
of the following year. While Louis XIV's interest
in the West Indies had waned, Charles II sent out a strong
force under Sir John Harman, which in June 1667 inflicted a
heavy naval defeat on the French off Martinique, effectively
regaining control of the Caribbean Sea.

An attack the same month on French-held St Kitts was
repelled with heavy losses, and thereafter the fleet was
recalled to Barbados by William Willoughby, no doubt,
following his brother's fate, from concern about the threat
of hurricanes. There, it was debated where next to strike.
Willoughby had one overriding priority – Suriname, only

two or three days' sailing from Bridgetown. But the soldiers and sailors, to be kept happy, needed booty. In the end, a plan was formulated to strike the French at Cayenne, where there would be rich pickings, then to retake Willoughbyland.

The fleet left Barbados on 10 August. Consisting of seven men-of-war, two ketches and two fireships, it carried some 850 soldiers. These were divided into two regiments of foot: one of 500 men under Colonel Philip Warner, a scion of the founding family of England's earliest West Indian colony of St. Kitts; the other of 350 men under Colonel Samuell Barry, a Barbadian. In overall command of the army contingent was the governor's son Lieutenant General Henry Willoughby. He seems to have been a thoughtful, experienced and well-organised officer. His orders for the attack on Cayenne are meticulous about discipline and aggression: his men were to hold fire with their muskets until within pistol range, then 'presse in upon the Enemy with the Clubb end of the Muskett and Sword'. Facing them, he was expecting 600 or 700 well-armed Frenchmen and a strong fort with forty cannon – intelligence that proved fairly accurate.

It did not all go to plan, of course. First, the element of surprise was lost when a French brigantine fell in among the fleet and, before action could be taken, raced off to warn the garrison at Cayenne. Then, even more seriously, a dead calm fell on the water. The fleet stopped. Days passed, then a week, almost without any movement. This brought 'many exigencies' for the soldiers, the greatest misery being from 'want of water'. 'Many fell downe sicke, & the rest very much weakened.'

When at last the wind returned, the attack swung into action. As per Henry Willoughby's plan, the leading assault troops were loaded into small schooners and longboats, with the former towing the latter, and headed for a wide bay overlooked by the town of Armyra on the other side of the island of Cayenne from its main fort. Only when they were half a mile from the shore, did they realise that there was a body of some 300 French troops drawn up at the water's edge at the leeward end of the bay. At once the English headed as fast as they could to the other end of the bay, while the French, spotting the boats, began a 'swift march' across the wide beach. At this, the troops in the longboats laid down their muskets and took up their oars to race against the French. When this was found to 'little avail', the pinnaces cut the tow ropes and headed off alone. Just under fifty men managed to reach the end of the bay before the leading French troops. The French commander, de Lézy, who was on the spot, ordered a volley, then 'according to the custom of their nation, to charge furiously'. The English returned fire, wounding both de Lézy and his second in command. At this moment the longboats hit the sand, and the rest of the

English advance party splashed ashore, at which point the French fell back.

Obeying their careful orders, the English restrained themselves from going in headlong pursuit, but instead advanced steadily towards the town of some sixty buildings. The French had retreated through it, and were now sitting out of musket range on high ground overlooking Armyra.

But after their long wait becalmed out at sea, the English troops now 'oppressed with violent thirst began to straggle from their officers & could not be reclaimed.' Their commander ordered them to draw up by the town's church, but nearby was a 'great store of merchandise and strong drink from which the soldiery could not be kept'. To regain control, the English commander ordered the town to be set alight and, at the same time, located a freshwater brook running into the sea. This might have been the time for the French to counter-attack, but the wounding of their leaders seems to have taken their heart, and they drew back to the main Cayenne settlement. The whole episode had lasted about fifteen minutes.

The next day, finding a small footpath along the coast, the English advanced towards Cayenne's fort, to be met by 'two French Gentlemen, the one a soldier, the other an inhabitant'. They carried a letter, explaining that their commander de Lézy had, the night before, 'repaired to his own house', collected all his money, plate and other valuables and with about 200 other inhabitants, including his second in command, had fled the colony in small boats, heading east towards Suriname. Hence, the fort was being surrendered. When they took possession, the English were astonished at the number of troops and the amount of provisions, arms and ammunition inside, more than enough, it seemed, to have kept them at bay.

Harman set about loading his ships with prisoners for ransom, artillery pieces from the French fort, and what was described as 'more plunder than will ever be known'. Before he left, he destroyed the fort and other strong buildings. The English had only lost two men, to the French twenty-three, and with the booty secured were ready for the retaking of Willoughbyland.

At four o'clock in the afternoon on 3 October 1667 Harman's fleet came within two leagues of the mouth of the Suriname river and dropped anchor. He was expected: de Lézy and his men from Cayenne had warned the Dutch and were now readying to fight the English alongside them.

The following morning, Harman's frigate, accompanied by two other men-of-war, and Henry Willoughby with some of his men in two ketches and a sloop, started upriver. Anchoring within sight of Fort Zeelandia, Willoughby sent two officers and a trumpeter in a pinnace with a letter demanding surrender, 'which if you refuse to do, you are to expect no favour but such as is summary in stormed places.'

Before it was within twice-musket range of the fort, the English pinnace was met by a Dutch boat, which forbade it from coming any nearer. When the English officer bearing the letter refused to hand it over to anyone but the governor, and the Dutch major made it clear that no Englishman was to be allowed anywhere near the defences, the two boats parted and returned their separate ways.

At dawn the next day, Willoughby's entire land force was put ashore half a mile downriver from the fort. But here the riverbank rose sharply and impassably, so to get nearer required a lengthy and exhausting detour through the thick forest. After trekking for more than two miles they came across a sugar works attached to a couple of small plantations about a mile from Paramaribo, where Henry Willoughby made his headquarters. From there he sent a small party forward to reconnoitre. When they came in sight of the town, they were fired on and one man was wounded. Returning to Willoughby, the scouts reported that the Dutch – or more exactly the pressed slaves – had been busy: the fort now had walls eighteen feet high, impossible to storm without ladders.

Orders came that evening from Sir John Harman that Willoughby's soldiers should harass the Dutch to 'keep the Enemy waking' and also endeavour to dam up the wells that lay outside the walls and constituted their only supply of fresh water. For his part, Harman promised to begin battering the fort from his ships as soon as the tide and wind permitted. So Willoughby split his forces, with Colonel Barry skirting round to the opposite side of the fort, and his own regiment creeping forward to within musket shot, while still remaining as far as possible under cover. All night, the Englishmen fired their muskets towards the fort, keeping the Dutch on constant alert.

The following morning, the naval bombardment began, with the English ships coming to anchor opposite the seaward walls of the fort and firing their cannons. At first they were able to deploy only their top tier of guns, but as the tide rose, so the ships could use the heavier cannons of their bottom tier also. While the infantrymen to the rear and sides of the fort poured small shot into it, in the hope of keeping the Dutch gunners' heads down, the English ships blasted away, several times clearing the ramparts of defenders. But the Dutch fired back with all the twenty-four guns they now had, hitting the English frigates hard, killing two captains, wounding another, and killing and wounding several dozen other officers and men.

Eventually, a flag of truce was raised on the fort's one remaining flag pole. But then nothing further happened. No men issued out under a flag of truce, so on their own initiative, a small body of English sailors swam or rowed to the bottom of the fort and, climbing on some debris that had been blasted from the top of the walls, entered the fort. At the same time, a handful of the infantrymen from the landward side did the same, and together they opened the gates and allowed the rest of the English soldiers to pour in. Inside, they found thirty-four of the 120-strong Dutch garrison lying dead as well as six of the French contingent; and the commander in high dudgeon that his fort had been stormed while he had his flag of truce out and was himself in his chamber writing out his terms of capitulation.

But the fort, the key to the colony, was back in English hands. Heading upriver, the victorious Henry Willoughby took possession of his late uncle's Parham Hill estate. Yet it appears that Willoughbyland remained extremely unhealthy, the new invaders quickly succumbing to infection. So leaving Colonel Barry as governor, with 100 men, Harman and his force departed without delay, to carry the news of the victory to William Willoughby in Barbados.

Willoughby's delight, however, was to be short-lived. Early the next month came devastating news from London. At the end of July, as William Scot had at least vaguely warned, de Ruyter had sailed up the Thames, then the Medway, and successfully attacked the Royal Navy's most important base at Chatham. More than a dozen ships were burnt and two, including the navy's flagship, the *Royal Charles*, were towed away. This humiliation quickly led to the signing of the Treaty of Breda, which ended the war.

During the treaty negotiations, the English commissioners Denzil Holles and Henry Coventry had offered to return New Netherland on the Hudson river in exchange for their sugar factories in Suriname. But with Francis Willoughby dead, Clarendon unpopular and on the brink of ruin, and opposition from the powerful Barbadian interest (who didn't want sugar competition), Suriname had few advocates. In addition, with its free trade and virtual independence, it lay outside the colonial system and was therefore of little benefit to the home country. Thus it was agreed that the combatants would hold on to their respective conquests as of 10 May that year, and Willoughbyland was effectively exchanged for what the English quickly renamed New York.

On 10 November 1667, a Zeeland frigate and six merchantmen arrived at Suriname, bringing with them news of the peace, and demanding the rendition of the colony. Barry delayed, responding that he could not surrender his charge without direct orders from his King or from William Willoughby. It seems, though, that he did begin looking at brokering a deal with the Dutch that would be to his own personal benefit.

Soon afterwards, Willoughby sent his son Henry back to Suriname to strip the colony bare. If he was to lose his inheritance, then he was determined to make sure that the Dutch took over a wasteland, 'so that [they] shall have little reason to glory of their purchase'. The English settlers there

A Maroon village. Escaped slaves overcame many difficulties and hardships to establish viable communities deep in the jungle, which have nevertheless always existed under some sort of threat. Ironically, they are the longest-lasting 'colonisers' of Suriname.

were urged to up sticks for Antigua and to take with them all their servants, slaves and movable belongings, including sugar machinery. Everything else was to be destroyed. Henry set the example by burning down the new sugar mill at Parham Hill. In the general chaos, hundreds of slaves escaped into the woods to form the nucleus of what would eventually become the largest Maroon (runaway slave) community in the world.

Some of the English, however, refused to leave, hoping that Charles II would change his mind. Henry departed, leaving Major James Banister – Behn's 'wild Irishman' – in charge, ordered to continue to persuade the English to relocate to one of the islands. Eventually, after imprisonment by the Dutch, in 1671 Banister led more than a hundred

Suriname families to Jamaica, taking with them over 400 slaves, twenty sugar kettles, cattle and wood. By then, Dutch protests had reached Charles II, who severely reprimanded William Willoughby for breaking the terms of the treaty. At last, the Dutch were in possession, and even persuaded a number of the 'raggedest' Englishmen to stay and help them re-establish the colony as a sugar producer.

Thus the English flag disappeared from the region for more than a century – after a period, from Ralegh onwards, of a succession of ambitious English enterprises. Aphra Behn in *Oroonoko* would lament, 'Had his late Majesty but seen and known what a vast and charming World he had been Master of in that Continent, he would never have parted so Easily with it to the Dutch.'

It was, in many ways, a poor deal. Suriname would become a sugar gold mine, generating vast profits for a tiny group of planters and their numerous Dutch backers, insurers, shippers and distillers. While the acquisition of New York closed the gap in English possessions along the American coastline and gave them command of the trade route from the Great Lakes, the sugar exports of Barbados alone remained more valuable than those of all of North America combined. Of course, New York was destined to become an important seaport and one of the world's great cities. But just over 100 years later it was no longer British. The Dutch held Suriname until 1975.

For Jonathan Atkins, the astute governor of Barbados in the 1670s, the failure of Willoughbyland was about one man's hubris and the collision of 'fantastical schemes' with harsh reality. There were simply not enough Englishmen in the West Indies to populate this vast region of South America. Francis Willoughby's 'schemes' were, in all, 'too much for any man's undertaking, though he had beene a prince considerable.'

In fact, Willoughby's huge financial investment in the colony was a key to its early success – unlike the previous English efforts, there were enough settlers to clear the land for crops and to keep the local people at bay. But thereafter his contribution is characterised by his absence from his domain and it would be left to others to decide by their actions whether the venture succeeded or failed. These pioneers brought with them their energy, ambition and dreams of a golden world, whether it be for a literally golden city, for a place of stunning commercial opportunity, for a haven of religious and political freedom, or for a 'lost world' of prelapsarian innocence. These hopes built the thriving, tolerant and cooperative colony of the 1650s.

But they also brought with them their greed, their squabbles from home, their appetites and, of course, after a while, slavery. In the end the gold of Willoughbyland would come not from the ground, but from the labour of enslaved Africans. With sugar established, profits poured in for the planters, but at the same time the community's unity fell apart, with its leaders split into rival factions and those at the bottom increasingly disgruntled and rebellious. The constant new threat of slave uprisings further destabilised the colony. The original hope of a golden world was lost, and when an external threat came in the form of the Dutch, few Englishmen thought the colony worth fighting for.

Thus the story of Willoughbyland's rise and fall is a microcosm of empire – its heady attractions and its fatal dangers. It also explores in miniature a pivotal moment in British and world history, when an original vision of white settlement, commonwealths of 'little Englands', was lost, replaced by racialised plantation societies, places of terror and cruelty, whose legacy is still with us today. As such its story shines a new light not just on the Caribbean sugar empire, but on all imperial ventures across the world.

POSTSCRIPT

'O Pangloss!' exclaimed Candide, 'you had
not guessed this abomination; this does it, at
last I shall have to renounce your optimism.'
'What is optimism?' said Cacambo.
'Alas,' said Candide, 'it is the mania of
maintaining that all is well when we are
miserable!' And he shed tears as he looked at
his Negro, and he entered Surinam weeping.'
VOLTAIRE, *CANDIDE*, 1759

Aphra Behn did not succeed in returning home from her
failed mission in Antwerp until May 1667. She had at
last secured a loan of £150 from a sympathetic fellow English
expatriate to pay what she owed to her lodging house, the Rosa
Noble. On her return, she may well have been imprisoned for
debt and released only on the condition that she undertake
another spying mission. Whether this happened or not is
unimportant: she had now set herself on the unprecedented
path – for a woman – of making money through her writing.

She would tell the story of Oroonoko to assembled friends and fellow scribblers many times, eventually writing it down in 1688, by which time she was famous for her dramas, wit and love affairs. She died the following year and was buried in Westminster Abbey under the name Astrea Behn.

William Scot's betrayal of Willoughbyland did not prevent him being cast aside by his new masters the Dutch. He was imprisoned for debt in The Hague in late 1666, and only released in early 1667 on the condition that he left the United Provinces for ever. He went to Antwerp, but after that is not heard of again.

William Byam, the villain of *Oroonoko*, relocated to Antigua following the demise of what he called 'our unfortunate colony of Surinam, war and pestilence having almost consumed it'. There he set about 'hewing a new fortune out of the woods', and secured marriage for his sons into the powerful Warner family, thereby establishing one of the richest and longest-lasting sugar-baron dynasties. He died in 1672.

James Banister, described by Behn as 'a fellow of absolute barbarity', joined Jamaica's council and was an important militia commander. By 1672 he owned 2,000 acres. In 1674, during a violent argument, he was murdered by the island's surveyor general, who was subsequently hanged. Jamaica was like that then.

Henry Willoughby established himself as a sugar planter in Barbados. In 1669, because of a disputed inheritance, he was murdered, poisoned by a rival, the famous sugar baron Christopher Codrington.

John Trefry remained in Suriname to the bitter end and beyond, dying there from fever in 1674. He stayed in touch with Aphra Behn until the end of his life.

In Suriname, William Willoughby's efforts to lure planters away had seen the colony visibly shrink in strength, with many fewer white men able to bear arms. According to Aphra Behn, a quarrel with the 'Indians', started by the English, became even more heated. The Dutch, she says, did not treat them 'so civilly as the English', so they 'cut in pieces all they cou'd take, getting into Houses, and hanging up the Mother, and all her Children about her; and cut a Footman, I left behind me, all in Joynts, and nail'd him to Trees.'

Indigenous 'Carib' leaders saw the chaos of the conquest as a chance to rid themselves of their new Dutch overlords and their 'Arawak' allies. In late 1678 they attacked European settlements across the colony, encouraging black slaves to rise up and wreck the mills. Massacres and fighting continued until troops shipped in from Holland re-established fragile control in 1681. By then, however, the number of runaway slaves, or Maroons, living in the interior was in the thousands.

The English had come to paradise, to a heaven, and left behind a hell. Dutch Suriname may have become a hugely profitable sugar-producing colony thanks in large part to the pioneering efforts of the English, but its reputation for cruelty, established by Byam and the English Cavalier adventurers, worsened.

As sugar production expanded, so did the number of slaves – there were some 22,000 by 1715, and 50,000 by 1735. Outnumbered twenty to one, and more in rural districts, the Dutch ruled by terror. The most trivial offences would be punished with a savage beating; insolence, running away or plotting rebellion brought torture and mutilation. Men, women and children were broken on the rack, burnt alive or hung by a hook through their ribs.

Unsurprisingly, the slaves responded by running away to join the Maroons, and then returning to extract vengeance. White planters were in their turn hooked on trees or roasted alive. Uprisings and their savage recriminations continued throughout the eighteenth century, on a scale greater even than Jamaica, Britain's most brutal slave colony.

By the time Voltaire came to write *Candide* in the 1750s, Suriname was considered perhaps the cruellest place in the world, famous for 'its heights of planter opulence and its depths of slave misery'. Voltaire's hero, wandering in South America, finds El Dorado almost by accident. Here there are no prisons, no religious discord and all food is provided for free by the government. Gold and jewels are so common as to be worthless. High mountains have protected it from the

The Execution of Breaking on the Rack.

Slave punishments in Suriname were famously cruel and, at the same time, ineffective in suppressing rebellion.

'rapaciousness' of the Europeans (although, the King reports, Ralegh had come close). For Voltaire then, El Dorado was not just about gold, but about innocence. It seems to Candide that he has found at last 'the country where all is well'.

However, his adventures immediately afterwards make an even bigger impression. He travels from El Dorado to Suriname, where he is robbed by a Dutch sea captain; he then meets a maimed slave who tells him, 'When we work in the sugar mills and the grindstone catches our fingers, they cut off the hand; when we try to run away, they cut off a leg. Both these things happened to me. This is the price paid for the sugar you eat in Europe.' It is a key moment for Candide: confronted with the horrors of slavery, he decides to renounce his optimism.

Like the English in Jamaica, the Dutch came to an agreement with a section of the Maroons, who had by now formed themselves into a number of 'tribes'. This effectively gave them independence and the free run of the inaccessible land beyond the cataracts, but wars continued. At one time in the late 1760s, the capital itself, now at Paramaribo, was threatened. The Dutch rushed some 1,200 troops to the colony, among whom was a Scottish mercenary, John Stedman. His account of his time there, *The Narrative of a Five Years Expedition against the Revolted Negroes of Surinam*, with help from illustrations by William Blake, became a

A nineteenth-century view of Paramaribo. Many of the elegant Dutch houses survive and the city is now a UNESCO heritage site.

classic anti-slavery text on a par with *Oroonoko*. He describes the lifestyles of the planters – characterised by extraordinary luxury, indulgence and drunkenness – and documents the brutal punishments inflicted on the slaves and captured Maroons. 'The colony of Surinam,' he wrote, 'is reeking and dyed with the blood of African negroes.' Unlike in the British colonies, where slavery was outlawed in 1838, in Suriname it only properly ended in 1873.

The city of El Dorado and its supposed lake continued to appear on maps of the area as late as 1808. In 1753 a Portuguese mercenary emerged from the Amazon jungle and described how, 'after a long and troublesome peregrination', he had seen the ruins of an ancient city from a mountain top. The man walked into the city, discovering 'stone arches, a statue, wide roads and a temple with hieroglyphics.'

The mercenary claimed, 'The ruins well showed the size and grandeur which must have been there and how populous and opulent it had been in the age in which it flourished.' Shortly afterwards, the Dutch West India Company sponsored a large expedition up the Essequibo river in search of the city, and the Portuguese in 1772 sent an armed party inland from the Amazon to lay claim to the area in which El Dorado was supposed to be located. When the Spanish heard of this, they sent troops from the Andes to drive them out. The two forces fought a bitter battle deep in Amazonia for possession of the mythical city. Only one Spaniard returned alive.

El Dorado retained its power as a literary fantasy, becoming popular subject matter for adventure stories for boys and adults. It also became a symbol of delusional greed. In Conrad's novella *Heart of Darkness*, the Eldorado Exploring Expedition journeys into the jungles of Africa in search of conquest and treasure, only to meet an untimely demise.

Searches for a real El Dorado continued well into the twentieth century, usually led by visionary eccentrics, and almost always disastrous for its personnel. One such man was Colonel Percy Fawcett, the gloriously moustached British explorer (and real-life model for Indiana Jones). In 1920 Fawcett – whose family motto was 'Difficulties be damned' – led a shambolic mission to find the lost city which ended when he had to shoot his horse (at a site known thereafter as Dead Horse Camp). Fawcett's expeditions often had this amateurish feel. He was known to leave for the jungle carrying only a sixty-pound backpack and a copy of Rudyard Kipling's poem 'The Explorer'. When his small party was ambushed by indigenous people, Fawcett is said to have ordered his men to play musical instruments and sing 'Soldiers of the Queen' while arrows landed around them.

In 1925 Fawcett, near destitute at the time, set out on his second expedition to find the city of gold. He was never seen again. In 1927 he was declared missing by the Royal Geographical Society. Two subsequent missions, one of which included Ian Fleming's brother Peter (from which resulted his classic *Brazilian Adventure*), attempted to find him, but with no success.

El Dorado has still not been located, although recent satellite photographs show intriguing geometrical shapes in the deep hinterland of Amazonia, which could be the remains of a lost city. Eventually the Guiana hills yielded some authentic gold, but it was no Klondike. Nevertheless, in the twentieth century, gold did become a significant export of the country, alongside lumber and bauxite. The most important mine today, Rosebel, is actually only a short distance from the site of Willoughby's Parham Hill.

Independence came in 1975, along with an offer of residency in the Netherlands if anyone wanted to leave.

About a third of the country, including most of its graduates and a lot of its capital-holders, took up the offer, leaving Suriname empty and poor. In the 1980s a military coup, political assassinations and a bitter war between the army and the Maroons made Suriname an international pariah. But the return of democracy has opened up the country once more to visitors.

I've searched far and wide for traces of Willoughbyland in Suriname. Behind me, at the beginning of my journey, lies the capital Paramaribo, which boasts some beautiful old wooden buildings, but they are firmly Dutch, and not even from the early period thanks to frequent fires in the city. Fort Zeelandia is still there, but substantially rebuilt. Perhaps, I muse, some of the stones at the base of the walls were laid by English hands to build Fort Willoughby.

At Parham Hill, there is a scattering of wooden huts from the slavery era, but they long post-date Willoughbyland. No one knows where on the site Willoughby built his house. I am shown a collection of bits and pieces dug up in the area – axe heads, metal cuffs and bottles, lots of bottles – but I can't imagine any of them are from Willoughby's time.

The oldest ruins still standing are at Joden Savanne, once the centre of the colony's thriving Jewish community. Here, half buried by forest, are more than 400 marble gravestones and the remains of the brick-built synagogue, the earliest of any architectural significance in the New World. The site is now eerily empty; the only living things I encounter are enormous busy ants and a sleepy tarantula. Anyway, the synagogue and almost all the graves are from after the Dutch takeover.

At the site of Torarica, once Willoughbyland's capital, there is no trace of the hundred or so houses or that this was once a place of human habitation at all. Instead a logging company is at work, felling huge trees hundreds of years old which have been growing where once there was a town square, warehouses, churches and a busy harbour.

So I head upriver, and at last after many more twists and bends and miles of hot, unrelenting jungle, I find something. But it is not a relic of the English colonists, or even the Dutch. Instead, it is the Africa the slaves were forced to leave behind.

On either side of the river now, we see black women washing clothes or pans in the water, and their children splashing about in the shallows. Here are the Maroons, the descendants of the runaway slaves. Back from the river, accessible only having passed through a 'spirit gate' of bamboo and leaves, crouch low wooden huts. At one of the villages we go ashore, and are shown around. Everyone wears brightly coloured printed shawls, and, it seems, all loads are carried on the head. Food comes from provision grounds cleared in the jungle by slash-and-burn, or from fish and bush meat still caught with spears and bows and arrows. Apart from the occasional mobile phone, there is little to distinguish the place from an African village of hundreds of years ago.

Here, as V. S. Naipaul wrote when he visited a Maroon village in the 1960s, the people 'have recreated Africa . . . [here they] have maintained their racial purity, their African arts of carving, singing and dancing, and, above all, their pride.'

So at last there is a glimpse of history that goes back to Willoughbyland. But it is not that of the plantation owners, their lavish estates and their cruel system. In fact, it is the reverse: instead of slavery it is rebellion-bought freedom and dignity that has endured.

ACKNOWLEDGEMENTS

As ever, I am much indebted to the scholars and academics who have written about this part of our history, in particular Sarah Barber, Laura Brown, Vincent Harlow, John Hemming, Peter Hulme, Joanna Lipking, Richard Price, James Rodway and James Williamson. I am also grateful to Maureen Duffy and Janet Todd for their excellent biographies of Aphra Behn.

Thanks go also to all those who have provided leads, encouragement or advice, or who have read and commented on earlier drafts: Professor Barbara Bush; Jessie Childs; Charlotte Crow; Adam Goodfellow; Liam Halligan; Miranda Kaufman; Geoff Lucas; Mathew Lyons; Sheila Parker; Professor Matthew Steggle; Paul Swain.

In Suriname, special thanks are owed to Noach Iagadeau, Sharishma Babel, Gabriel van Ommeren and Hilde Neus. I'm also grateful to Sheila Parker for her help in translating French sources, and to Martinette Susijn, who translated from the Dutch, and to all those who work in the various archives I have consulted, in particular the staff of the Rare Books and Manuscripts reading rooms at the British Library and Sarah Butler at the University of Leeds.

Special thanks to Laura Susijn, a friend when in need, to Martin Brown, for his ever-clear and handsome maps, and to Emmy Lopes for her beautiful redrawing of the 1667 map.

As before I have been lucky to have a wonderful publishing team at Hutchinson, in particular my brilliant editor Sarah Rigby. I am also grateful for the work of copyeditor Mary Chamberlain, proofreader Sarah-Jane Forder, designer Rich Carr and indexer Alison Worthington. Thanks also go to my agents Julian Alexander in London and George Lucas in New York. My greatest debt, however, is to my family and in particular to Hannah, *mi gaang mati.*

LIST OF ILLUSTRATIONS

Integrated Pictures and Maps

1. The Caribbean, Guiana and the Spanish Main, 1650. Drawn by Martin Brown; © Hutchinson 2015.

2. Rivers of the Wild Coast. Drawn by Martin Brown; © Hutchinson 2015.

3. Ritual gilding of El Dorado by Theodor De Bry, late 1500s. Topham Picturepoint.

4. Ralegh with Topiawari. British Library Board/TopFoto.

5. Manoa, or El Dorado, 1599. Topham Picturepoint.

6. San Thomé, 1617. From *Ralegh's Last Voyage*, ed. Vincent Harlow, 1932.

7. Jewish Savannah, early 1700s. From P. J. Benoit, *Voyage à Surinam: description des possessions néerlandaises dans la Guyane*, 1839.

8. Francis Lord Willoughby during the Civil War. TopFoto.

9. Map of Barbados. From Richard Ligon, *A True and Exact History of the Island of Barbados*, 1657.

10. Huntsman spider and pinktoe tarantula. From Maria Sybilla Merian, *Metamorphosis Insectorum Surinamensium of de Verandering der Surinaamsche Insecten*, 1705. © The Natural History Museum/Alamy.

11. Indigenous inhabitants of Suriname. From P. J. Benoit, *Voyage à Surinam: description des possessions néerlandaises dans la Guyane*, 1839. Widener Library, HCL, Harvard University.

12. Giant anaconda. From John Stedman, *Expedition to Surinam, Being the Narrative of a Five Years Expedition against the Revolted Negroes of Surinam*, 1796. © The Art Archive/Alamy.

13. A Description of the Colony of Surranam in Guiana, 1667. Redrawn by Emmy Lopes; © Hutchinson 2015.

14. Aphra Behn, sketched by George Scharf. Public domain.

15. Indigenous Surinamese. From P. J. Benoit, *Voyage à Surinam: description des possessions néerlandaises dans la Guyane*, 1839. Widener Library, HCL, Harvard University.

Colour Pictures

SOURCE NOTES

Abbreviations

BL   British Library, London
Bod   Bodleian Library, Oxford
Cal. Dom. Calendar of State Papers. Domestic Series
Cal. Col. Calendar of State Papers. Colonial Series (America and the West Indies)
CUP   Cambridge University Press
DNB   Dictionary of National Biography
EHR   English Historical Review
HMC   Historical Manuscripts Commission
JBMHS *Journal of the Barbados Museum and Historical Society*
PRO   Public Record Office, Kew
OUP   Oxford University Press
UNCP   University of North Carolina Press
YUP   Yale University Press

One: 'Every Man's Longing'

3: 'There is a way found to answer every man's longing', Ralegh, *The Discoverie*, ed. Harlow, 6 (quotation page numbers from this edition).

4: 'Eternal Spring ...', Behn, *Oroonoko*, 43 (quotations from Norton Critical Edition, ed. Joanna Lipking, 1997).

4: 'strange rarities, both of beasts, fish ...', report by Renatus Enys, Cal. Col. 1661– 8, no. 577, 166–7.

5: 'shall be by him enjoyed and kept without any disturbance ...', BL Add. MSS 11411, f. 95ff; Cal. Col. Addenda 1574–1674, no. 199, 86.

8: 'the sweetest place that was ever seen; delicate rivers ...', Francis Willoughby to his wife, quoted in Schomburgk, *The History of Barbados*, 275.

8: 'that hath yet her Maidenhead . . .', Ralegh, *The Discoverie*, 73.

Two: El Dorado

9: 'What do you not drive human hearts into, cursed craving for gold!', Virgil, *The Aeneid*, III, 56.

10: 'thorough-shining, and marvellous rich … hath more abundance of gold than any part of Peru', Ralegh, *The Discoverie*, 7, 17.

12: 'asked whether the things we saw were not a dream', Carrasco, David (ed.), *The History of the Conquest of New Spain by Bernal Diaz de Castillo*. Albuquerque: University of New Mexico Press, 2009, 156.

15: 'conquer such another land as [he] himself had found …', Ralegh, *The Discoverie*, ed. Harlow, introduction, liii.

16: 'a very sterile and pestilential land, with very few natives . . . Their hair fell out, and in its place emerged a pestilential scabies …', quoted in Hemming, *The Search for El Dorado*, 146.

16: 'The reports are false. There is nothing on the river but despair', Nicholl, *The Creature in the Map*, 28.

17: In 1549, the governor of Hispaniola commissioned a Spanish nobleman …, Ralegh, *The Discoverie*, ed. Harlow, introduction, lxvii.

17: 'loose ten or a dozen arrows …', Jean-Baptiste Labat, *Nouveau Voyage aux isles de l'Amérique*. Paris: La Haye, 1724, 112.

19: 'May it please God to let this concealed province be discovered … ', quoted in Hemming, *The Search for El Dorado*, 167.

20: 'does not and never did have foundations', Ralegh, *The Discoverie*, ed. Harlow, introduction, lxxvii.

21: 'great towns and a vast population with gold and precious stones', ibid., lxxxi–ii.

22: 'I know not whether the silver-smiths of Spain …', ibid., lxxiii–iv.

Three: Ralegh and the 'Beautiful Empire of Guiana'

23: 'one of the most extraordinary men that ever appeared', Raynal, *A Philosophical and Political History*, 251.

24: 'who had offended many and was maligned of most', quoted in Lyons, *The Favourite*, 5.

24: 'discover, settle and govern any lands not already in the possession of a Christian Prince', Ralegh, *The Discoverie*, introduction, xl.

25: 'that endangereth and disturbeth all the nations of Europe', ibid., 9.

25: He might have been told about it by Pedro Sarmiento de Gamboa …, Lyons, *The Favourite*, 304.

26: 'a man most honest and valiant', Ralegh, *The Discoverie*, 13.

26: two from Trinidad and two from the mainland, to be trained as interpreters …, Vaughan, *Transatlantic Encounters*, 30.

28: 'was stricken into a great melancholy and sadness', Ralegh, *The Discoverie*, 34.

28: 'broken lands and drowned lands', ibid., 37.

29: 'the most beautiful country that ever mine eyes beheld', ibid., 42.

29: 'by violence or otherwise, ever knew any of their women …' ibid., 44.

30: 'I marvelled to find a man of that gravity and judgement …' ibid., 52.

32: an 'Indian Prince' in a 'devise', Vaughan, *Transatlantic Encounters*, 33.

32: 'who was desirous to tarry, and could describe a country with his pen', Ralegh, *The Discoverie*, 63.

33: 'hath more quantity of gold, by manifold, than the best parts of the Indies, or Peru', Ralegh, ibid., 5.

33: too 'easeful and sensual', ibid., 4.

35: 'I can discern no sufficient impediment to the contrary…', Hakluyt, *The Principal Navigations*, vol. x, 488–9.

35: 'in the winter of my life, [I] undertake these travails fitter for bodies less blasted with misfortune', Ralegh, *The Discoverie*, 3.

35: 'in the excessive taking thereof they exceed all nations', ibid., 39.

36: 'cruel and bloodthirsty … feast, dance, and drink of their wines in abundance', ibid., 26.

36: 'all places yield an abundance of cotton, of silk, of balsamum . . .', ibid., 72.

36: 'large coats and hats of crimson colour', ibid., 51.

37: 'be very likely that the emperor [of El Dorado] hath build and erected as magnificent palaces in Guiana as his ancestors did in Peru', ibid., 71.

37: 'had the maidenhead of Peru', Ralegh, *The Discoverie*, 9.

37: 'hath yet her Maidenhead . . . never sacked, turned, nor wrought …', ibid., 73.

Four: The Heirs of Ralegh

41: 'All young gentlemen, soldiers and others that live at home in idleness …', Harcourt, *A Relation of a Voyage to Guiana*, 131.

41: 'that upper rich country', Hakluyt, *The Principal Navigations*, vol. x, 452.

43: the Spanish lived in a state of constant siege, virtually unable to leave the fort …, report by A. Cabeliau in Harlow, *Ralegh's Last Voyage*, 128.

43: the whole coast remained 'unconquered', Buddingh', *De Geschiedenis van Suriname*, 14.

44: 'departed from Woolwich with the intention to discover …', 'Captaine Charles Leigh his voyage to Guiana and plantation there', in Purchas, *His Pilgrimes*, vol. xvi, 309.

44: 'blue-headed parrots', ibid., 310.

45: 'the best humoured Indians of America …', Major John Scott, 'The Discription of Guyana', BL Sloane MSS 3662, f. 39.

45: 'saying he promised to have returned to them before that time', 'The Relation of Master John Wilson of Wansteed in Essex, one of the last ten that returned into England from Wiapoco in Guiana 1606', in Purchas, *His Pilgrimes*, vol. xvi, 350.

45: the other was called Pluainma …, Leigh account, Purchas, *His Pilgrimes*, vol. xvi, 315.

46: 'so much discontented that they cried to their Captaine, "Home, Home"', Wilson account, ibid., 338.

46: 'for spoyle and purchase', Leigh account, ibid., 318.

47: 'mutinors and monstrous sailors', Leigh account, ibid., 322.

47: the 'Indians were not so kind to us as they had promised', Leigh account, ibid., 312.

48: 'very weak and much changed', Wilson account, ibid., 339.

49: 'which were heartily welcome to my hungry company', Harcourt, *A Relation of a Voyage to Guiana*, 71.

49: 'Indians . . . expressed much joy and contentment . . .', ibid., 72.

50: '. . . he died a Christian, yea a Christian of England', ibid., 147.

50: 'to their remembrance the exploits of Sir Walter Raleigh', ibid., 73.

50: 'a loving, tractable, and gentle people, affecting and preferring the English before all nations whatsoever', ibid., 113.

50: 'exceeding rich, never yet broken up . . . but still remains in the greatest perfection of fertility', Rodway and Thomas, *Chronological History of the Discovery and Settlement of Guiana*, 60.

50: 'in search of those Golden Mountains, promised unto us before the beginning of our voyage', Harcourt, *A Relation of a Voyage to Guiana*, 107.

52: 'more fit to have been confined in a mad house than to govern a colony', ibid., 112.

Five: Ralegh's Last Voyage

56: 'I found by experience false', Harlow, *Ralegh's Last Voyage*, 11.

58: 'the scum of men', ibid., 52.

60: 'unadvised daringness', ibid., 60.

62: Keymis asked if that was Ralegh's 'resolution; I told him it was . . .', 'Sir Walter Raghleys Large Appologie for the ill successe of his enterprise to Guiana', in Harlow, *Ralegh's Last Voyage*, 328.

62: 'My brains are broken and 'tis a torment for me to write . . .', letter 22 March 1617, BL Add. MSS 34631, f. 47.

63: 'It was my full intent to go for gold, for the benefit of his Majesty and the rest of my countrymen', *The Works of Sir Walter Ralegh*, Oxford: OUP, 1829, vol. 1, 694.

64: 'the site of the country and people so contented them . . .', Harlow (ed.), *Colonising Expeditions*, lxxvii.

65: 'sometimes dying stark mad, sometimes their bowels breaking out of their bodies . . .', Ralegh, *The Discovery of Guiana*, 49.

65: 'river of Surenama' as 'the best part of all that tract of land . . .', 'Sir Walter Raghleys Large Appologie', in Harlow, *Ralegh's Last Voyage*, 323.

65: According to a notarial deed from 1617, Buddingh', *De Geschiedenis van Suriname*, 14.

66: In an account from the 1660s there is a mention of Frenchmen being 'cut off' . . ., Scott, 'The Discription of Guyana', BL Sloane MSS 3662, f. 40b.

66: Another account suggests that the French fort was instead built by an expedition . . ., Biet, *Voyage de la France Equinoxiale en L'Isle de Cayenne*, 261.

67: There are also sketchy Jewish records of settlement in Suriname that go back to 1639 ..., Rev. J. S. Roos, 'Additional Notes on the History of the Jews in Surinam', *Publications of the American Jewish Historical Society*, No. 13, 1928, 128.

68: Captain Marshall seems to have come from Barbados ..., Arbell, *The Jewish Nation of the Caribbean*, 82–3.

68: 'want of supplies' and the hostility of the local 'Carribees', 'The Discription of Tobago', BL Sloane MSS 3662, f. 48.

68: 'a flourishing community of three hundred English families', Harlow, *Colonising Expeditions*, lxxxvii.

68: 'they espoused the quarrel of the French and were cut off by the natives', Scott, 'The Discription of Guyana', BL Sloane MSS 3662, f. 40b.

68: 'little other welcome than a resting place for their bones', Harlow, *Colonising Expeditions*, lviii.

Six: Francis Lord Willoughby

69: Francis Willoughby would be described by contemporaries as both charming and self-centred ..., Spalding, *Contemporaries of Bulstrode Whitelocke*, 246.

71: 'to bring him in some wenches', BL Harleian MSS 165, f. 280r.

72: 'We are all hasting to an early ruin. Nobility and gentry are going down apace', quoted from HMC 4th report, 268, by Barber, 'Power in the English Caribbean', 191.

73: 'one of the richest spots of earth under the sun', Ligon, *A True and Exact History of the Island of Barbados*, 86.

76: in 1643 the planters in Barbados used the chaos of the Civil War quietly to stop paying proprietorial dues ..., Richard Dunn, *Sugar and Slaves: the Rise of the Planter Class in the English West Indies, 1624–1713*. Chapel Hill, NC: UNCP, 1972, 79.

76: eventually appealing successfully to the Commons for redress ..., Roy E. Schreiber, 'The First Carlisle: Sir James Hay, First Earl of Carlisle, as Courtier, Diplomat and Entrepreneur, 1580–1636', *Transactions of the American Philosophical Society*, Volume 74, Part 7, 182.

76: 'Lieutenant-General of the Charibbee Islands, for the better settling and securing them', Cal. Col., 26 February 1647, 327.

76: For four months they remained imprisoned without charge ..., Spalding, *Contemporaries of Bulstrode Whitelocke*, 478.

77: 'Since all is gone at home, it is time to provide elsewhere for a being', Cary, *Memorials of the Great Civil War*, vol. 2, 313.

78: 'against the king we are resolved never to be ...', Bell to Hay, 21 July 1645, quoted in Bridenbaughs, *No Peace beyond the Line*, 158.

80: 'he was once a Roundhead, and might be again', 'A.B.', *A Brief relation of the beginning and ending of the troubles of the Barbados*. London, 1653, 5.

80: 'the trumpeters receiving money and as much wine as they could drink', Cal. Col. 1574–1660, 22 November 1650, no. 25, 345.

80: 'politic conduct', Schomburgk, *The History of Barbados*, 271.

80: 'welcomed as a blessing from God', Barber, 'Power in the English Caribbean', 193.

81: 'For the People's freedom against all tyrants whatsoever', DNB

81: 'an ugly rascal' and a 'whore-monger', 'Documents and letters in the Brotherton Collection relating to Barbados', JMBHS vol. 24, no. 4 (1956–7), 175.

81: 'a great lover of pretty girls ...', John Aubrey, *Brief Lives*, ed. Richard Barber. Woodbridge: Boydell and Brewer, 1975, 195.

81: a member 'whose immorality is a disgrace to the house', 'Documents and letters in the Brotherton Collection', 180n.

82: 'to prevent all misunderstanding and to settle a perfect and free trade with them', Harlow, *A History of Barbados*, 60.

82: offering pretty much anything in return for being allowed to do business in Barbados with the Dutch ..., PRO SPCol 1/11/23, 20 November 1650.

82: Barbadians 'looked on themselves as a free people', Barber, *A Revolutionary Rogue: Henry Marten and the English Republic*, 126.

82: 'to renounce all obedience to Charles Stuart, and acknowledge the supreme authority of the present Parliament', Cal. Col. 1574–1660, no. 25, 346.

82: 'If ever they get this island, it shall cost them more than it is worth before they have it', Schomburgk, *The History of Barbados*, 274.

84: 'my very kind and loyal friend a person of as much honesty and courtesy as I have ever met with in these parts', letter of 9 July 1656 George Marten to Henry Marten, 'Documents and letters in the Brotherton Collection', 186.

84: 'a Gentleman of great Gallantrie and Prudence and of Long Experience in ye West Indies', Scott, 'The Discription of Guyana', BL Sloane MSS 3662, f. 40b.

85: 'being man-eaters, and very false in performing their promises', *A Collection of voyages and travels, Consisting of Authentic Writers in our own Tongue*, London, 1745, vol. 2, 754.

85: 'reviving the name of Sir Walter Raleigh gave the English firm footing in those parts', Scott, 'The Discription of Guyana', BL Sloane MSS 3662, f. 40b.

85: 'the air to be so pure, and the water so good ...', Schomburgk, *The History of Barbados*, 274–5.

86: Jacob Enoch, a Dutch Jew, living a little way upriver with his family ..., Oxenbridge, *A Seasonable Proposition*, 7.

86: to 'receive' the English to 'settle amongst them', Schomburgk, *The History of Barbados*, 274–5.

86: 'in a few years to have many thousands there', ibid., 275.

87: 'He has delivered us from the Lord Willoughby ...', letter from George Marten to Henry Marten, 29 March 1652, 'Documents and letters in the Brotherton Collection, 182.

88: 'so long as he submits to the authority of the Commonwealth', Cal. Col.
    1574–1660, 7 January 1652, 371.

88: 'Ordered to quit the island', Cal. Col. 1574–1660, 3 June 1662, no. 53,
    380.

Seven: 'A Brave Land'

89: 'flowers and trees of such variety as were sufficient to make ten volumes of
    Herbals', Ralegh, *The Discoverie*, 40.

90: 'It is almost as easy to enumerate the stars of heaven ...', Warren, *An
    Impartial Description of Surinam*, 8–10.

90: such novelties for the arriving Europeans as manatees, 'swordfish', caiman
    and giant otters ..., ibid., 2.

90: 'yet be always finding some creature or other he had not met withal before',
    ibid., 15.

90: 'that a man can hardly hear himself speak ...', ibid., 22.

92: 'The heat,' one newcomer wrote, 'is something violent', ibid., 3.

93: 'the English are very well established here', Biet, *Voyage de la France
    Equinoxiale*, 266.

93: 'nothing more beautiful in the world', ibid., 261.

94: 'a worthy gentleman, in heart and word', ibid., 263.

95: 'much craftier, and subtler than the Negroes; and in their nature falser',
    Ligon, *A True and Exact History of the Island of Barbados*, 54.

96: According to an account from the 1660s, there were some 5,000 'Carreeb' ...,
    Scott, 'The Discription of Guyana', BL Sloane MSS 3662, ff. 38, 40b.

96: 'they colour themselves all over into neat works ...', Warren, *An Impartial
    Description of Surinam*, 23-4.

96: 'Indians are great lovers of fine gardens, drinking, dancing, and divers other
    pleasures', Scott, 'The Discription of Guyana', BL Sloane MSS 3662, f.
    40b. f. 38.

97: 'for defence . . . shields made of light wood, handsomely painted and
    engraved', Warren, *An Impartial Description of Surinam*, 26.

97: 'with the most barbarous cruelties', ibid., 26.

97: there is a fleeting reference in one source to assaults on the first English
    settlers ..., ibid., 26.

97: 'were always frustrated, and they profoundly smarted for their folly', ibid.,
    23.

98: 'we find it absolutely necessary to caress them as friends, and not to treat
    'em as slaves ...', Behn, *Oroonoko*, 10.

98: 'for trifles', Warren, *An Impartial Description of Surinam*, 26.

98: French priest Antoine Biet noted the presence of indigenous household
    slaves ..., Biet, *Voyage de la France Equinoxiale*, 267.

98: the locals remained 'very useful', Behn, *Oroonoko*, 11.

99: 'truly good, and nearly resembles our strongest March-Beer ...', Warren,
    An Impartial Description of Surinam, 7.

99: 'Gods of the rivers ... so rare an art they have in swimming, diving and almost living in the water', Behn, *Oroonoko*, 11.

99: 'that they may not hurt the fruit', ibid., 11.

99: 'excellently favoured', Ralegh, *The Discoverie*, 46.

100: 'was of excellent shape and colour, for it was a pure bright bay...' Ligon, *A True and Exact History of the Island of Barbados*, 54.

101: 'straggling from the rest, was met by this Indian maid ...', ibid., 55.

101: 'chanced to be with child, by a Christian servant', ibid., 54.

102: up to 600 men as well as women and children by December 1654 ..., *A Collection of the State Papers of John Thurloe Esq.*, London, 1742, vol. 3, 63.

102: 'perfect peace with the Indians ... flourishing condition', Scott, 'The Discription of Guyana', BL Sloane MSS 3662, f. 41.

102: 'treachery of James I ... and the base dullness of that age', PRO CO 1/11, f. 118v.

102: 'It is a brave tract of land ...' Cal. Col. 1574–1660, 16 February 1662, no. 41, 374.

102: 'that from thence a strength may be easily conveyed into the bowels of the Spaniard at Peru', 'Reasons Offered by the Lord Willoughby why Hee Ought Not to be Confined in his Settlement upon Serranam', BL Egerton MSS 2395, f. 281; 'Certaine Overtures Made by Ye Lord Willoughby ...', BL Sloane MSS 159, ff. 21–21b.

104: 'having overcome the hardship and great difficulty of a new settlement', BL Egerton MSS 2395, f. 281b.

Eight: 'A Peculiar Form of Government'

105: 'You shall live freely there, without serjeants ...', *Eastward Hoe*, Manchester: Manchester University Press ed., 1999, 138.

105: 'The delights of warm countries are mingled with sharp sauces', Warren, *An Impartial Description of Surinam*, A2.

106: 'to expel those moist humours, which such tempers in that country do abundantly contract', ibid., 4.

106: 'a certain sweating disease' that first caused numbness to the joints, followed by a burning fever ..., Scott, 'The Discription of Guyana', BL Sloane MSS 3662, f. 38.

106: 'most loathsome and not easily cur'd mischief', Warren, *An Impartial Description of Surinam*, 4.

106: 'Things there Venomous and Hurtful', ibid., 20–2.

109: 'with his Head and Shoulders eaten off', ibid., 13.

109: 'blessings and advantages are of far greater weight' than any of these threats ..., ibid., 21.

109: the colony was 'daily increasing', Scott, 'The Discription of Guyana', BL Sloane MSS 3662, f. 41.

109: a white population of some 26,000 ..., Bridenbaughs, *No Peace beyond the Line*, 226.

111: 'to make this place a free state, and not run any fortune with England, either in peace or war', 'Documents and letters in the Brotherton Collection', 188.

111: In March 1654 the Council in London had recommended that letters patent ..., Cal. Col. 1574–1660, 16 March 1664, 414.

112: living in Barbados in 1661 ..., Sanford, *Surinam Justice*, 50.

112: 'any person authorized in the government amongst them', A *Collection of the State Papers of John Thurloe Esq.*, vol. 6, 391.

112: an assembly of twenty-one men ..., Sanford, *Surinam Justice*, 45.

113: 'peculiar kind of Government ... elective in the people', Cal. Col. 1661–8, no. 351, 104.

113: In 1658 he abandoned Barbados for Willoughbyland ..., Barber, A *Revolutionary Rogue*, 135.

114: a synagogue (the first of which was built in 1654) ..., Barber, 'Power in the English Caribbean', 204.

115: space for numerous ships – of up to 300 tons – to anchor ..., Warren, An *Impartial Description of Surinam*, 1.

115: 'to be ready upon any great occasion', DNB.

116: on condition that he give security of £10,000 and remove himself to Suriname ..., Cal. Col. 1574–1660, 26 November 1657, 461.

117: 'see my country freed from that intolerable slavery ...', Tanner, *English Constitutional Conflicts*, 207.

117: the most successful Guiana colony yet with over a thousand settlers ..., Cal. Col. 1661–8, 7 May 1661, no. 83, 28.

Nine: The Restoration: 'A Tumbling and Rolling World'

119: 'O England, England, England, England, what hast thou done?', 'Yet One Warning More, to Thee O England', London, 1660, 29, quoted in Greaves, *Deliver Us from Evil*, 210.

119: 'so joyful a day and so bright ever seen in this nation', quoted in Tanner, *English Constitutional Conflicts*, 209.

120: Other pamphleteers had demanded the disestablishment of the Church ..., ibid., 214.

121: some 300 treasonous books or pamphlets ..., Greaves, *Deliver Us from Evil*, 209.

123: he was reinstated to the plum position of Royal Governor of the 'Caribbees' ..., Cal. Col. 1574–1660, 483.

123: 'great grievance to the inhabitants to be given away from the Crown', Cal. Col. 1574–1660, 16 July 1660, 483.

124: letters patent from the King were issued ..., Cal. Col. 1661–8, 6 May 1663, no. 451, 131–2.

125: 'free trade, without custom', Cal. Col. 1661–8, no. 209, 66.

125: 'It is most certain that there is both gold, silver and emerald ...', Major John Scott, 'The Historical and Geographicall Description of the Great

River of the Amazons ... and of the several Nations inhabiting that famous Country', Bod, Rawlinson MSS 'A' 175, f. 355.

126: 'The Indians will tell you of mighty Princes upwards ...', Warren, *An Impartial Description of Surinam*, A2.

126: 'With most grievous labour ... were at last, compell'd to return without desired Success ...', ibid., 3.

126: 'because all the Country was mad to be going on this Golden Adventure', Behn, *Oroonoko*, 51.

127: 'Our colony is daily improving ...', Trefry to Charles Pym, 15 August 1662, HMC, 10th report, part vi (Bouverie MSS), 96.

127: 'thirty or forty pounds a ton', Harcourt, *A Relation of a Voyage to Guiana*, 44.

128: 'Rich gums, balsoms, many Phisickall Drugs', Scott, 'The Discription of Guyana', BL Sloane MSS 3662, f. 37b.

128: *Mercurious Publicus* informed its English readership, 30 May 1662.

129: 'our sugar is far better, and of greater price than that of Barbados', Trefry to Charles Pym, 15 August 1662, HMC, 10th report, part vi (Bouverie MSS), 96.

129: a claim repeated by Enys and Warren ..., Cal. Col. 1661–8, no. 577, 167; Warren, *An Impartial Description of Surinam*, 16–17.

132: more profit than 'is usually produc'd from a greater foundation, and more ...', ibid., 18.

132: 'their hypocrisies are discovered, and several families are transporting thither', Renatus Enys, Cal. Col. 1661–8, no. 577, 167.

132: 'liberty to such as inhabit said province and cannot conform to the Church of England', Cal. Col. 1661–8, 6 May 1663, no. 451, 131.

132: Petitions from 1661 show a good number arriving then ..., Arbell, *The Jewish Nation of the Caribbean*, 83.

133: 'have, with their persons and property, proved themselves useful ...', *Publications of the American Jewish Historical Society*, vol. 9, 1901, p144–6.

134: 'here in greater plenty and variety than in England or any of its Plantations elsewhere settled', Oxenbridge, *A Seasonable Proposition*, 9.

135: 'lascivious Abominations', 'bitter oaths and horrid execrations', Adis, *A Letter Sent from Syrranam*, 3–5.

135: more 'civilly bred ... All new colonies you know of what sort of people generally they are made up of', ibid., 7.

136: 'good order, being nobly upheld by the power and prudence of those at the helm ...', Renatus Enys, Cal. Col. 1661–8, no. 577, 167.

Ten: Repression and Revolt

137: 'abusing the authority of the colony' and for his 'insufferable insolence', Sanford, *Surinam Justice*, 2–3.

137: William Sanford was a member of the council and his brother Robert ..., Warren, *An Impartial Description of Surinam*, 6.

138: 'peculiar kind of Government ... elective in the people', Cal. Col. 1661–8, 3 September 1662, no. 363, 108.

139: 'pretendeth to have his Majesty's proclamation, but never showeth it ...', Sanford, *Surinam Justice*, 1–2.

139: 'the generality, robbed of their privileges ...', Cal. Col., 1661–8, 17 August 1662, no. 351, 104.

139: '... hazards life, and fortunes to enlarge his Majesty's dominions ...', Sanford, *Surinam Justice*, A4.

140: Byam only cancelled the election because he knew he was going to lose, Sanford alleged ..., ibid., 9.

140: Both sides accused the other of 'sloth and drunkenness'..., ibid., 6.

140: 'did very insolently spit in the face of authority', ibid., 4.

140: 'usurpt', 'arbitrary and tyrannical', ibid., A3.

140: 'garrisoning his house' and putting 'parties in boats upon the river', ibid., 9.

140: 'seize my person', ibid., 15.

141: 'vomited such pickled language as exceeded the rhetoric of Billingsgate', ibid., 18.

141: 'disputed Byam's authority' were also seized, 'many asleep in the beds', by 'parties of musketeers', Sanford appeal to the Privy Council, August 1662. BL Add. MSS 29587, f. 79.

142: was responsible for the outrage of the bones of sixteenth-century Anglican archbishop Matthew Parker ..., Spencer, *Killers of the King*, 122.

143: 'I do not repent of any thing I have done; if it were to do, I could do it again', ibid., 106.

146: 'no society or scarce family [was] found empty of an informer', Sanford, *Surinam Justice*, 9.

Eleven: Aphra Behn, Agent 160

147: 'of a generous and open temper, something passionate', 'The History of the Life and Memoirs of Mrs. Behn', published in *All the Histories and Novels Written by the Late Ingenious Mrs. Behn, Entire in One Volume*, 1698, 2.

149: 'a reproach to her womanhood ...', preface to Cal. Dom. 1666–67, published in 1864, xxvii.

149: 'shady and amorous . . . she who earned them the right to speak their minds', Virginia Woolf, *A Room of One's Own*. London: Hogarth Press, 1929, 95.

151: Killigrew was friends with Willoughby and had sons with plantations in the West Indies ..., Todd, *The Secret Life of Aphra Behn*, 73n.

152: 'An account of his Affairs there', 'The History of the Life and Memoirs of Mrs. Behn', 3.

153: 'the Sense of Smelling which may, at any time, enjoy a full delight ...', Warren, *An Impartial Description of Surinam*, 5.

154: 'so perfect a Meander, that in a matter of fifteen Leagues' sailing ...', ibid., 2.

154: 'continues as far as hath been discover'd', ibid., 1.

154: 'for ought is known', ibid., 3.

154: 'very thriving stock of cattle', Byam letter, HMC, Manuscripts of the Duke of Portland at Welbeck vol. 3, 308.

154: 'vast Rock of white Marble' ... 'softest Murmurs and Purlings' ... even to the finest gardens of 'boasted Italy', Behn, *Oroonoko*, 44.

155: 'by nature there are rare, delightful and wonderful', ibid., 8.

156: 'a brave Country ... no place is more accommodate ...', Warren, *An Impartial Description of Surinam*, A2.

156: 'vast Extent', reaching 'one way as far as China ... eternal spring, always the very Months of April, May and June', Behn, *Oroonoko*, 43

156: 'very sickly, and apt to fall into Fits of dangerous Illness', ibid., 64

156: 'Tigers' in the jungle, and 'numb eels' in the rivers, ibid., 46.

156: 'so brave a man .... wise and eloquent ...', ibid., 58.

157: 'Slaves for four years' – were all 'overtaken in drink', ibid., 51.

157: 'such notorious Villains as Newgate never transported ...', ibid., 59.

157: 'the most fawning fair-tongu'd fellow in the world ...', ibid., 54.

158: 'a wild Irishman ... a fellow of absolute barbarity ...' , ibid., 64.

158: 'a man of great gallantry wit and goodness', ibid., 57.

158: 'resolved to espouse all distress or felicities of fortune', Byam to Harley, 14 March 1664, Portland Collection, University of Nottingham Department of Manuscripts, Pw2 Hy221, quoted in Duffy, *The Passionate Shepherdess*, 48.

159: 'three or four dozen glass bottles of excellent Canary ...', GM to HM, 29 March 1652, 'Documents and letters in the Brotherton Collection', 186.

159: 'Methinks my Soul is grown more gay and vigorous ...', *The Young King*, Act 3, Scene 1.

160: 'rogue', Cal. Dom. 1666–7, 27 August 1666, no. 38, 72.

Twelve: Sugar, Slavery and *Oroonoko*

162: 'treat with the natives ...', Cal. Col. 1661–8, 16 June 1663, no. 489, 142.

162: 'happy people as to this world ...', Warren, *An Impartial Description of Surinam*, 23–4.

163: 'like our first Parents before the Fall', Behn, *Oroonoko*, 9.

163: 'About this time we were in many mortal Fears ...', ibid., 47.

163: 'they set up a loud cry, that frighted us at first ...', ibid., 48.

163: 'beads, bits of tin ... and any shining trinket', ibid., 9.

164: 'infinitely surprising to them', ibid., 48.

165: 'so good an understanding between the Indians and the English ...', ibid., 50.

166: as early as 1653 had a slave population of 20,000, supplied in the main by Dutch traders ..., Bridenbaughs, *No Peace beyond the Line*, 226.

167: ... fittingly, the *Charles* and the *James* ..., Joanna Lipking, 'The New World of Slavery: An Introduction', in *Oroonoko*, Norton Critical ed., 80.

168: 'A guinea man arrived here in this river … She has 130 nigroes on board', letter of 27 January 1663 to Sir Robert Harley from William Yearworth, HMC, Portland, vol. 3, 280.

168: Aphra Behn, who left Suriname soon afterwards …, Behn, *Oroonoko*, 11.

168: 'Those then whom we make use of to work in our plantations of sugar, are negro's …', ibid., 11.

168: 'for help with in labour, you may more easily than in cold Countries …', Oxenbridge, *A Seasonable Proposition*, 10.

169: as many as 3,000 enslaved Africans in the colony …, Jan Voorhoeve and Ursy M. Lichtveld (eds), *Creole Drum: An Anthology of Creole Literature in Surinam*, New Haven: YUP, 1975, 3.

171: 'Of the Negroes, Or Slaves' … that indeed unequalled slavery', Warren, *An Impartial Description of Surinam*, 19–20.

171: 'Mutinies – which is very fatal sometimes in those colonies, that abound so with Slaves', Behn, *Oroonoko*, 41.

172: 'was one of those places in which they found the most advantageous Trading …', ibid., 11.

173: 'the most beautiful that ever had been seen', ibid., 18–19.

173: and 'a vast quantity of slaves', ibid., 41.

175: 'We were all (but Caesar) afflicted by this news', ibid., 63.

177: 'he gave up the Ghost, without a groan, or a reproach', ibid., 64.

177: 'who refused it; and swore, he had rather see the quarters of Banister …', ibid., 65.

178: 'She helped to prepare literary people's minds …', Hugh Thomas, *The Slave Trade*, London: Picador, 1997, 452

178: Oroonoko himself is a slave trader; when he first meets Imoinda he presents her with 150 slaves 'in fetters', Behn, *Oroonoko*, 14.

179: he seems, unusually, to have let his workers live together as families …, Barber, *A Revolutionary Rogue*, 131.

179: Behn was 'Europeanising' him for her English readers …, Todd, *The Secret Life of Aphra Behn*, 136.

180: 'without the unattractive flat nose or that large mouth that the other blacks have', Joanna Lipking, 'The New World of Slavery – An Introduction', 77.

180: some high-status Africans did, like Oroonoko, have European tutors …, Davis, *The Problem of Slavery in Western Culture*, 477.

180: 'ancient Gold Coast negro', Anon, *Great Newes from the Barbadoes*, London, 1676, 10.

180: 'redeemed by a merchant in London', W.J. Cameron, 'New Light on Aphra Behn', University of Auckland monograph, 1961, 7.

180: 'a circumstance that affected the audience yet more than the play …', quoted in Brown, *Ends of Empire*, 25–6.

181: a 'Coraomantien' known as Jermes had established …, Price, *The Guiana Maroons*, 23.

181: 'desperate attempts for the recovery of their liberty', Warren, *An Impartial Description of Surinam*, 19.

181: 'the insolent disorder of our own Negroes', Byam, 'An Exact Narrative of Ye State of Guyana & of the English Colony in Surynam in Ye Beginning of Ye Warre with Ye Dutch & of its Actions During the Warre, and the Taking Thereof by a Fleet from Zeeland', Bod, Ashmolean MSS, ff. 109–122, and BL Sloane MSS 3662, ff. 32b–49, in Harlow, *Colonising Expeditions*, 221.

181: 'I need not enlarge but to advise you of the sympathetical passion ...', Portland Collection, University of Nottingham Department of Manuscripts, Pw2 Hy221, quoted in Duffy, *The Passionate Shepherdess*, 48

182: The initials of Grand Shepherd Celadon are the same as Scot's ..., Duffy, *The Passionate Shepherdess*, 50.

Thirteen: The Return of Willoughby

183: 'On the sudden/A Roman thought hath struck him', *Antony and Cleopatra*, Act 1, Scene 2

183: 'What cares these roarers for the name of king?', *The Tempest*, Act 1, Scene 1

183: 'Under God being the foundation and essence of this colony', quoted in Barber, 'Power in the English Caribbean', 208.

184: 'bottomed by royal authority', Renatus Enys, Cal. Col. 1661–8, no. 577, 166.

184: 'to the inexpressible joy of all the Inhabitants', Byam, *An Exact Relation of the Most Execrable Attempts of John Allin*, 3.

184: 'there was some difference between the inhabitants and his Lordship', Scott, 'The Discription of Guyana', BL Sloane MSS 3662, f. 41.

184: Allin was one of a number, a faction ..., Cal. Col. 1661–8, 16 March 1666, no. 1,152, 368.

185: 'no subject could be a Lord Proprietor as it infringed the liberty of the subject ...', Rodway and Watt. *Chronological History of the Discovery and Settlement of Guiana*, 167.

186: 'negro coat', Byam, *An Exact Relation*, 10.

187: 'talk to the rabble, and not to him', ibid., 10.

187: was 'seized with internal tortures, and in a short time became senseless and expired', ibid., 11.

187: 'I have too much of the Roman in me ...', ibid., 8–9

188: 'and when dry-barbicued or dry-roasted ...', ibid., 11.

189: 'strange jealousies' and 'great discontents', Byam, 'An Exact Narrative ...', in Harlow, *Colonising Expeditions*, 200.

189: 'a most strange violent Feavor, burning within ...' 'swept many away', ibid., 203, 199

Fourteen: War and Ruin

192: 'recognised carriers of Europe', Henry L. Schoolcraft, 'The Capture of New Amsterdam', EHR vol. 22, no. 88, 1907, 674.

193: 'the trade of the world is too little for us two, therefore one must down', Pepys Diary, 2 February 1664.

194: Stuyvesant surrendered the colony on 8 September ..., Schoolcraft, 'The Capture of New Amsterdam', EHR vol. 22, no. 88, 1907, 674ff.

195: '1,500 lusty fellows', Cal. Col. 1661–8, 10 August 1664, no. 786, .222.

195: 'the good old Colonel leaping out of the boat ...', Cal. Col. 1661–8, 16 November 1665, no. 1,085, 329.

195: 'When the Dutch have lost one or two small islands more ...', Cal. Col. 1661–8, 3 November 1665, no. 1,073, 326.

196: 'in its meridian and after this month had its declination and went ever retrograde', Byam, 'An Exact Narrative', in Harlow, *Colonising Expeditions*, 199.

198: There were, however, as per Willoughby's instructions, six guns mounted ..., ibid., 200.

198: 'root the Dutch out of all places in the West Indies', Cal. Col. 1661–8, 16 November 1665, no. 1,082, 329.

198: 'one of the most picturesque and far-wandering scoundrels of his time', Wilbur C. Abbot, *Colonel John Scott of Long Island*, New Haven: YUP, 1918, preface.

199: 'a poor bankrupt miller's wife', ibid., 4.

199: his notorious 'smooth tongue', ibid., 67.

200: 'burnt and destroyed the enemy's towns, goods ...', Cal. Col. 1661–8, no. 1,525, 481.

200: leaving small garrisons at Pomeroon ..., Byam, 'An Exact Narrative', in Harlow, *Colonising Expeditions*, 200.

200: 'not at that time in a Condition to offend, nor well to defend itself[~]', ibid., 201.

203: 'utterly destroying the whole Colony', ibid., 203.

Fifteen: Astrea and Celadon

205: 'Consider, then, my beautiful Astrea ...', Honoré d'Urfé, *L'Astrée*, translated by Steven Rendall, Tempe, Arizona: Medieval & Renaissance Texts & Studies, 1997, book 1, 18.

205: by August it had killed 200 men 'and very many women and children', Byam, 'An Exact Narrative', in Harlow, *Colonising Expeditions*, 203.

205: with six barrels of powder and some 'match', ibid., 204.

207: a 'violent storm', letter from Captain William Porter to Sir Robert Harley, 11 October 1666, HMC, Portland, vol. 3, 300.

208: 'ye dismall news of ye Burning of London', Byam, 'An Exact Narrative', in Harlow, *Colonising Expeditions*, 204.

208: He set lookouts in canoes at the river mouth ..., ibid., 204–5.

210: Scot hoped in return for 'a large sum for his secret'..., Duffy, *The Passionate Shepherdess*, 69.

211: William Scot was now on a retainer of 1,000 rixdollars a year from Dutch leader de Witt ..., Cal. Dom. 1664–5, 3 August 1665, no. 15, 500.

211: 'son of Thos. Scot, executed for high treason', Cal. Dom. 1665–6, 26 March 1666, no. 24, 318.

212: the 'speckled plumes' were much admired, Todd, *The Secret Life of Aphra Behn*, 73.

212: 'Unusual with my Sex, or to my Years', Malcolm Hicks (ed.), *Aphra Behn: Selected Poems*, New York: Routledge, 2003, 61.

215: it seems that Arlington and Killigrew were happy to wring out of Scot ..., Duffy, *The Passionate Shepherdess*, 92.

215: 'serve the King as his lawful sovereign', Cal. Dom. 1666–7, 21 September 1666, no. 81, 145.

216: 'believed in him all things', quoted in Duffy, *The Passionate Shepherdess*, 85.

216: 'fool him so long ...', Cal. Dom. 1666–7, 3 November 1666, no. 42, 236.

Sixteen: The Fall of Fort Willoughby

219: 'In February arrived a Dutch fleet from Zealand ...', William Byam to Sir Robert Harley, 6 November 1668, HMC, Portland, vol. 3, 308.

219: In addition to the regular crew of about 750 sailors ..., Wolbers, *Geschiedenis Van Suriname*, 40.

220: 'take the English by surprise' and to 'seek fortune', Jos Fontaine, *Zeelandia: De Geschiedenis van een Fort*, 15.

220: 'courageous sealions', Wolbers, *Geschiedenis Van Suriname*, 40.

220: scooping up the ships – one Irish and one from New England ..., Byam, 'An Exact Narrative', in Harlow, *Colonising Expeditions*, 206.

221: 'sent orders into the country', ibid., 205.

221: 'half a fort', ibid., 205.

221: The 'most serviceable gun', ibid., 206.

222: Byam had only a hundred men, ibid., 206.

222: had shrunk to 700 by July, ibid., 221.

222: Now a full-scale epidemic, the fever had carried off 500 by the beginning of 1667, Byam letter, HMC, Portland, vol. 3, 310

222: 200 were too sick or lame to be able to fight, Byam, 'An Exact Narrative', in Harlow, *Colonising Expeditions*, 203, 211.

223: 'Miserable were ye Cryes, & dejected were ye Spirits of all', ibid., 203.

223: 'weak & exceeding lame', ibid., 204.

223: 'stript his colours and refused to fight, and some of the soldiers also', ibid., 210.

223: to 'establish a community free from aristocratic tendencies', Rev. A. Hilfman, 'Notes on the History of the Jews in Surinam', *Publications of the American Jewish Historical Society*, vol. 18, 1909, 181.

224: 'against all opposers; and so you might act your hostility as soon as you please', Cal. Col. 1661–8, 24 February 1667, no. 1,421, 448.

225: 'the enemy commanded from their decks and quarter deck ...', Byam, 'An Exact Narrative', in Harlow, *Colonising Expeditions*, 208.

226: some 700 equipped with scaling ladders and grenades ..., Byam letter, HMC, Portland, vol. 3, 308.

227: 'most immediately clave to the Dutch', ibid., 308

227: 'promised to show them every creek and corner ...', Byam, 'An Exact Narrative', in Harlow, *Colonising Expeditions*, 209.

227: 'A big blessed victory!', 'True Story of the Glorious Conquest of Pirmeriba ...', 29 May 1667, in Fontaine, *Zeelandia: De Geschiedenis van een Fort*, 21–3.

227: 'the most beautiful river of the entire coast has been conquered ...', ibid., 23.

228: Byam's account of what occurred next is somewhat confused ..., Byam, 'An Exact Narrative', in Harlow, *Colonising Expeditions*, 210–12.

229: Joseph Nassy, had already accepted a position ..., Wolbers, *Geschiedenis Van Suriname*, 40–1.

229: 'Christian servants and persons dishonest and in debt ...', 'From ye Honoble Lt Gen Willm Byam & the rest of ye Councell to his Exey Francis Willoughby of Parham, the humble Address of Representacon of ye Assembly being ye representative Body of ye Colony of Surynam', in Harlow, *Colonising Expeditions*, 213.

230: 'hourly expected ... who will effect such mischiefe as will consequently produce the ruining of us all', ibid., 213.

230: 'very thriving stock of cattle at St Johns', Byam letter, HMC, Portland, vol. 3, 308.

231: Fifteen pieces of artillery and a hundred and twenty men ..., Wolbers, *Geschiedenis Van Suriname*, 40–1.

231: 'pitifully surrendered without resistance' to a load of 'brewers and cheesemongers', Bod, Clarendon MSS, vol. 84, ff. 177–8.

232: Prompted by Robert Sanford, Byam's old 'inveterate and malicious enemy', Byam letter, HMC, Portland, vol. 3, 309.

Seventeen: Victory and Anguish

234: 'presse in upon the Enemy with the Clubb end of the Muskett and Sword', 'An Exact Narrative Concerninge the takeinge the Island of Cayenne from the French, & the Fort & Collony of Surrynam from the Dutch July 1667', PRO CO 1/19, no. 90, f. 173b.

235: 'Many fell downe sicke, & the rest very much weakened', ibid., f. 176.

237: de Lézy and his men from Cayenne had warned the Dutch ..., Wolbers, *Geschiedenis Van Suriname*, 40–2.

237: 'which if you refuse to do, you are to expect no favour ...', 'An Exact Narrative Concerninge the takeinge the Island of Cayenne ...', f. 182b.

238: 'keep the Enemy waking', ibid., f. 185.

240: Inside, they found thirty-four of the 120-strong Dutch garrison lying dead ..., Wolbers, *Geschiedenis Van Suriname*, 40.

241: 'so that [they] shall have little reason to glory of their purchase', Cal. Col. 1661–8, 2–9 March 1668, no. 1,710, 552.

242: Henry set the example by burning down the new sugar mill at Parham Hill ..., Cal. Col. 1661–88, no. 1,746 (iv), 567.

243: taking with them over 400 slaves ..., Cal. Col. 1661–8, 4 June 1668, no. 1,759, 571.

243: 'Had his late Majesty but seen and known what a vast and charming World ...', Behn, *Oroonoko*, 43.

244: 'too much for any man's undertaking ...', PRO CO 1/37, no. 22, July 1676.

Postscript

248: about 'hewing a new fortune out of the woods', Byam letter, HMC, Portland, vol. 3, 309.

249: 'so civilly as the English', so they 'cut in pieces all they cou'd take ...', Behn, *Oroonoko*, 47.

250: 22,000 by 1715, and 50,000 by 1735 ..., Price, *The Guiana Maroons*, 7.

250: 'its heights of planter opulence and its depths of slave misery', Stedman, *Expedition to Surinam*, Prices ed., xiii.

253: 'The colony of Surinam,' he wrote, 'is reeking and dyed with the blood of African negroes', Stedman, *Expedition to Surinam*, Folio Society ed., v.

258: 'have recreated Africa ... [here they] have maintained their racial purity ...', Naipaul, *Middle Passage*, 175.

SELECT BIBLIOGRAPHY
OF PRINTED SOURCES

Adis, Henry. *A Letter Sent from Syrranam*. London: 1664

Amussen, Susan Dwyer. *Caribbean Exchanges: Slavery and the Transformation of English Society, 1640–1700*. Chapel Hill, N.C.: UNCP, 2007

Anon. *Bloudy Newes from the Barbadoes*. London: 1652

Anon. *Interesting Tracts, Relating to the Island of Jamaica*. St Jago de la Vega, Jamaica: Lewis, Lunan and Jones, 1800

Arbell, Mordechai. *The Jewish Nation of the Caribbean: The Spanish–Portuguese Jewish Settlements in the Caribbean and the Guianas*. Jerusalem: Gefen Publishing House, 2002

Armitage, D. *The Ideological Roots of the British Empire*. Cambridge: CUP, 2000

Bailyn, Bernard and Morgan, Philip D. *Strangers within the Realm: Cultural Margins of the First British Empire*. Chapel Hill, N.C.: UNCP, 1991

Barber, Sarah. *A Revolutionary Rogue: Henry Marten and the English Republic*. Sutton: Stroud, 2000

Barber, Sarah. 'Power in the English Caribbean: The Proprietorship of Lord Willoughby of Parham' in L. H. Roper and B. Van Ruymbeke, eds. *Constructing Early Modern Empires: Proprietary Ventures in the Atlantic World, 1500–1750*. Leiden: Brill, 2007

Behn, Aphra. *Oroonoko: or the Royal Slave, A true History*. London: Will. Canning, 1688

Biet, Antoine. *Voyage de la France Equinoxiale en L'Isle de Cayenne*. Paris: 1664

Bridenbaughs, Carl and Roberta. *No Peace beyond the Line: The English in the Caribbean, 1624–1690*. New York: OUP, 1972

Brown, Enid. *Suriname and the Netherlands Antilles: an annotated English-language Bibliography*. London: Scarecrow Press, 1992

Brown, Laura. *Ends of Empire: Woman and Ideology in Early Eighteenth-century English Literature*. New York: Cornell University Press, 1993

Buddingh', Hans. *De Geschiedenis van Suriname*. Utrecht: Unieboek Het Spectrum, 1999

Byam, William. *An Exact Relation of the Most Execrable Attempts of John Allin, Committed on the Person of His Excellency Francis Lord Willoughby*. London: 1665

Canny, Nicholas P., ed. *The Origins of Empire*. Oxford: OUP, 1998

Cary, Henry, ed. *Memorials of the Great Civil War in England from 1646 to 1652*. 2 vols, London: 1842

Davis, David Brion. *The Problem of Slavery in Western Culture*. New York: Cornell University Press, 1966

Deerr, Noel. *The History of Sugar*. 2 vols, London: Chapman and Hall, 1949–50

Duffy, Maureen. *The Passionate Shepherdess: The Life of Aphra Behn*. London: Jonathan Cape, 1977

Fontaine, Jos. *Zeelandia: De Geschiedenis van een Fort*. Zutphen: De Walburg Pers, 1972

Foster, Nicholas. *A Briefe relation of the late Horrid Rebellion Acted in the Island of Barbados*. London: 1650

Gimlette, John. *Wild Coast: Travels on South America's Untamed Edge*. London: Profile Books, 2011

Goreau, Angeline. *Reconstructing Aphra: A Social Biography of Aphra Behn*. Oxford: OUP, 1980

Goslinga, Cornelius. *A Short History of Netherlands Antilles & Surinam*. The Hague: Nijhoff, 1879

—*The Dutch in the Caribbean and on the Wild Coast, 1580–1680*. Gainesville: University of Florida Press, 1971

Greaves, Richard L. *Deliver Us from Evil: The Radical Underground in Britain, 1660–1663*. Oxford: OUP, 1986

Greenblatt, Stephen, ed. *New World Encounters*. Berkeley: UCLA Press, 1995

Habib, Imtiaz. *Black Lives in the British Archives, 1500–1677*. Aldershot: Ashgate, 2008

Hakluyt, Richard. *The Principal Navigations, Voyages, Traffiques and Discoveries of the English Nation*. Edinburgh: E. & G. Goldsmid, 1884–90

Harcourt, Robert. *A Relation of a Voyage to Guiana*. London: 1613

Haring, C. H. *The Buccaneers in the West Indies in the XVII Century*. London: Methuen & Co., 1910

Harlow, Vincent T. *A History of Barbados, 1625–1685*. Oxford: Clarendon Press, 1926

—ed. *The Voyage of Captain William Jackson, 1624–1645*. London: Royal Historical Society, 1923

—ed. *The Voyage of Captain William Jackson, 1624–1645*. London: Royal Historical Society, 1923

—ed. *Colonising Expeditions to the West Indies and Guiana, 1623–1667*. London: Hakluyt Society, 1925

—ed. *The Discoverie of the Large and bewtiful Empire of Guiana*. London: Argonaut Press, 1928

—*Ralegh's Last Voyage*. London: Argonaut Press, 1932

Harris, C. A., ed. *Harcourt's Relation of a Voyage to Guiana*. London: Hakluyt Society, 1928

Hartsinck, Jan Jacob. *Beschryving Van Guiana, of de Wilde Kust in Zuid-America*. Amsterdam: Gerrit Tielenburg, 1770

Hemming, John. *The Search for El Dorado*. London: Michael Joseph, 1978

Hendricks, Margo and Parker, Patricia, eds. *Women, 'Race,' and Writing in the Early Modern Period*. London: Routledge, 1994

Hibbert, Christopher. *Cavaliers and Roundheads*. London: HarperCollins, 1993

Hill, Christopher. *God's Englishman: Oliver Cromwell and the English Revolution*. London: Weidenfeld & Nicolson, 1970

Hill, J. D., ed. *History, Power, and Identity: Ethnogenesis in the Americas*. Iowa: University of Iowa Press, 1996

Hopper, Andrew. *Turncoats and Renegadoes*. Oxford: OUP, 2012

Hulme, Peter. *Colonial Encounters: Europe and the Native Caribbean*. London: Methuen, 1986

Hulme, Peter. *Wild Majesty: Encounters with Caribs from Columbus to the Present Day, An Anthology*. Oxford: Clarendon Press, 1992

Israel, Jonathan I. *Dutch Primacy in World Trade, 1585–1740*. Oxford: Clarendon Press, 1989

Iwanisziw, Susan B. *Oroonoko: Adaptations and Offshoots*. Aldershot: Ashgate, 2006

Jesse, Rev. C. 'Barbadians Buy St. Lucia from the Caribs: the Sale of St. Lucia by Indian Warner and Other Caribs to the Barbadians in A.D. 1663.' *JBMHS* 32:4 (November 1968): 180–6

Krise, Thomas W., ed. *Caribbeana: An Anthology of English Literature of the West Indies, 1657–1777*. Chicago: University of Chicago Press, 1999

Kriz, Kay Dian. *Slavery, Sugar and the Culture of Refinement*. New Haven, Conn.: YUP, 2008

Ligon, Richard. *A True and Exact History of the Island of Barbados*. London: 1657

Lyons, Mathew. *The Favourite: Ralegh and his Queen*. London: Constable, 2011

Menard, Russell R. *Sweet Negotiations: Sugar, Slavery, and Plantation Agriculture in Early Barbados*. Charlottesville and London: University of Virginia Press, 2006

Mintz, Sidney W. *Sweetness and Power: The Place of Sugar in Modern History*. New York: Penguin, 1985

Naipaul, V. S. *The Loss of El Dorado*. London: Andre Deutsch, 1969

—*The Middle Passage: Impressions of Five Societies – British, French and Dutch – in the West Indies and South America*. London: Andre Deutsch, 1962

Nassy, David de Ishak Cohen, et al. *Essai Historique sur la Colonie de Surinam*. Paramaribo: 1788

Nicholl, Charles. *The Creature in the Map*. London: Jonathan Cape, 1995

Nussbaum, Felicity, and Brown, Laura, eds. *The New Eighteenth Century*. London: Methuen, 1987

Oldmixon, John. *The British Empire in America*. 2 vols, London: 1708

Oxenbridge, John. *A Seasonable Proposition of Propagating the Gospel . . .* London: 1670

Parker, Matthew. *The Sugar Barons*. London: Hutchinson, 2011

Pepys, Samuel. *The Diary of Samuel Pepys*. London: Sonnenschein & Co., 1890

Pestana, Carla Gardina. *The English Atlantic in an Age of Revolution, 1640–1661*. Cambridge, Mass.: HUP, 2004

Phaf-Rheinberger, Ineke. *The 'Air of Liberty': Narratives of the South Atlantic Past*. Amsterdam: Rodopi, 2008

Picard, Liza. *Restoration London*. London: Weidenfeld & Nicolson, 1997

Price, Richard. *Maroon Societies: Rebel Slave Communities in the Americas*. New York: Anchor Books, 1973

Price, Richard. *The Guiana Maroons*. Baltimore: Johns Hopkins University Press, 1976

Puckrein, Gary. *Little England: Plantation Society and Anglo-Barbadian Politics, 1627–1700*. New York: New York University Press, 1984

Purchas, Samuel. *His Pilgrimes*. Glasgow: Maclehose, 1905–7

Ralegh, Sir Walter. *The Discoverie of the Large, Rich and Bewtiful Empyre of Guiana . . .* London: 1596

Raynal, Guillaume-Thomas-François. *A Philosophical and Political History of the Settlements and Trade of the Europeans in the East and West Indies*. Vol. 4, Edinburgh: 1776

Richardson, Bonham C. *The Caribbean in the Wider World, 1492–1992: A Regional Geography*. Cambridge: CUP, 1992

Rodger, N. A. M. *The Command of the Ocean: A Naval History of Britain Volume Two 1649–1815*. London: Allen Lane, 2004

Rodway, James and Watt, Thomas. *Chronological History of the Discovery and Settlement of Guiana, 1493–1668*. Georgetown: Royal Gazette Office, 1888

Rodway, James. *Guiana: British, Dutch, and French*. London: T. Fisher Unwin, 1912

Sanford, Robert. *Surinam Justice*. London: 1662

Schomburgk, Sir Robert H. *The History of Barbados*. London: Longman, Brown, Green and Longmans, 1848

Schwartz, Stuart B., ed. *Tropical Babylons: Sugar and the Making of the Atlantic World, 1450–1680*. Chapel Hill, N.C.: UNCP, 2004

Spalding, Ruth. *Contemporaries of Bulstrode Whitelocke 1605–1675*. Oxford: OUP, 1989

Spalding, Ruth, ed. *The Diary of Bulstrode Whitelocke, 1605–1675*. Oxford: OUP, 1989

Spencer, Charles. *Killers of the King*. London: Bloomsbury, 2014

Stedman, John. *Expedition to Surinam, Being the Narrative of a Five Years Expedition against the Revolted Negroes of Surinam*. Reprinted London: Folio Society, 1963

Tanner, J. R. *English Constitutional Conflicts of the Seventeenth Century*. Cambridge: CUP, 1928

Thornton, A. P. *West Indian Policy Under the Restoration*. Oxford: Clarendon Press, 1956

Todd, Janet. *The Secret Life of Aphra Behn*. London: Pandora, 2000

Vaughan, Alden T. *Transatlantic Encounters: American Indians in Britain, 1500–1776*. Cambridge: CUP, 2006

Wallace, Willard M. *Sir Walter Raleigh*. London: OUP, 1959

Warnsinck, J. C. M. Abraham. *Crijnssen De Verovering Van Suriname En Zijn Aanslag Op Virginië*. Amsterdam: NV. Noord-Hollandsche Uitgeversmaatschappij, 1936

Warren, George. *An Impartial Description of Surinam upon the Continent of Guiana in America*. London: 1667

Westoll, Andrew. *Surinam: Stumbling through the Dark Heart of South America's Forgotten Jungle*. London: Old Street Publishing, 2009

Williamson, James A. *The English in Guiana and on the Amazon*. Oxford: Clarendon Press, 1923

Wolbers, J. *Geschiedenis Van Suriname*. Amsterdam: H. De Hoogh, 1861

INDEX

MAR 2 2 2018